Viction

Viction

Where Vision and Action Collide

V **A** **ICTION**

VICTION
WHERE VISION AND ACTION COLLIDE

Sherry Chester

Copyright © 2020 by Sherry Chester.

Library of Congress Control Number: 2020905777
ISBN: Hardcover   978-1-7960-9583-8
          Softcover   978-1-7960-9582-1
          eBook   978-1-7960-9581-4

All rights reserved. No part of this book may be reproduced or transmitted in any form or by any means, electronic or mechanical, including photocopying, recording, or by any information storage and retrieval system, without permission in writing from the copyright owner.

Any people depicted in stock imagery provided by Getty Images are models, and such images are being used for illustrative purposes only.
Certain stock imagery © Getty Images.

Unless otherwise indicated, all Scripture quotations are from The Holy Bible, English Standard Version® (ESV®), copyright © 2001 by Crossway. Used by permission. All rights reserved.

Print information available on the last page.

Rev. date: 03/28/2020

To order additional copies of this book, contact:
Xlibris
1-888-795-4274
www.Xlibris.com
Orders@Xlibris.com
807017

DEVOTED DEDICATION TO THE MOST HIGH GOD

Forever Father
whose extravagant love I have known since childhood and will forever more.

Honoring Husband
whose protective covering as Kinsman Redeemer is the lover of my soul.

Faithful Friend
whose unconditional love, company, and conversation I embrace with great joy.

ENDEARING ENDORSEMENTS

This refreshing book by Sherry is sure to sharpen you and help you grow as a leader. Whether you need a total re-set for your ministry, feel like you have hit a ceiling in your service or simply want to be more effective, you will find much distilled wisdom in this book. It does not provide a simplistic 'three steps instant success,' but rather it gives a guide to building a strong ministry from the ground up with the right foundation and divine focus so that your fruit will last. Be encouraged as you read to step to the next level of serving Jesus and those He has placed around you.
Olly Goldenberg,
FOUNDER of CHILDREN CAN
www.childrencan.co.uk

What an inspirational delight it has been reading Sherry Chester's new book on *Viction, Where Vision and Action Collide* purposefully. Sherry has included such excellent, insightful and yet common-sense leadership skills, that any leader in the home, work place, or ministry can advance their visions, dreams and goals. As you read you can make great personal assessments of where you are right now in your leadership skill development and learn sound Biblical steps for your own personal growth, as well as new insight in gaining greater leadership capabilities. I highly recommend investing your time in reading, studying and applying the principles in this well written life improvement book.
Douglas J. Wingate, Ph.D.

President and Founder of Life Christian University
www.lcus.edu

Today's leaders must be more than just planners, visionaries, or task managers, but must be able to pair their vision with action. In her latest work, *Viction: Where Vision and Action Collide*, Sherry Chester has masterfully articulated how effective ministries are those that move beyond simply maintaining church programs. This resource will give strategic solutions to not only equip your leadership but will also deepen your own faith in the process. It is a must read for any Children's Ministry leader that is desperate for a greater intimacy with God. Sherry reminds us that a Children's Ministry is only as healthy as its leader. Chester equips you with the right tools that are sure to catapult you and your Children's Ministry to the next level. You and your leadership team will be equipped with effective strategies, courage, confidence, and passion to overcome complacency and continue to strive to fulfill the call of God on your life to reach the next generation for Christ.

Esther Moreno - Founder & CEO
Child's Heart Ministries
Huntsville, Alabama
www.childsheart83.com

Sherry shares good basic reminders of what it takes to be the best Christian leader you can be whether you are a children's ministry leader or any type of leader.

Becky Fischer
Kids in Ministry International
http://kidsinministry.org

How does a leadership book manage to be greatly inspirational, yet extremely practical? I am not sure how, but Sherry Chester accomplished that in this book *Viction: Where Vision and Action Collide*. How I wish someone had imparted this wisdom and practical advice to me years ago! Sherry has given a gift to new and seasoned leaders through her deeply personal stories and easy to read format. This handbook is one to be referred to again and again.

Connie McKenzie
Director Children & Family Ministries
Christ For The Nations, Dallas, TX
www.cfni.org and www.kidsforthenations.com

In *Viction: Where Vision and Action Collide*, Sherry Chester delivers her insights on moving your thoughts from ideas to intentional world-changing movements. Regardless of status or position, everyone must recognize the tactics the enemy uses in attacking your thought life. Sherry pulls back the curtain for us all to see what is required to take our thoughts captive and the steps we need to begin believing and acting on the word of God.

Corey Jones
NextGen Pastor
Southern Hills, the Church at City Station

If you want to put action to your vision, read this book. *Viction* provides practical, intentional, and strategic ways to bring your vision to life. Sherry creates compelling calls-to-action in a relational leadership style that makes you believe you can do it!

Trish Weeks
Kidmin Nation Mega-Con Conference Director
Ministry Coach & Relational Leadership

Sherry is one of the most passionate people God so graciously brought into my faith journey. With great enthusiasm, a constant desire to learn, a willingness to share her knowledge and experiences, and her ability to build a team that forges into children's ministry in unity, make Sherry a model in the kidmin world. She listens for God's direction, and on more than one occasion has stepped in to offer me encouragement at the perfect moment. Now, as she ventures into this new way of delivering light and help when there is darkness and questions, I am confident you will glean from what Sherry has to share.

Tina Houser
Author of Children's Ministry Resources
Tinahouser.net

In a day and age that the word "leader and influencer" have become so flippant with social media expansion. God is looking for those who will actually yield their lives to be His leader. It is one thing to be seen as a leader in the world but quite different when it comes to biblical leadership! I think this book will give great insight to the narrative written over your life as well as keys to help those of you who are growing into the leader God has called you to be! I would highly recommend anything from Sherry Chester. When it comes to a fruitful life with God, her life screams of that. I have always said, "don't follow someone without a story of trials and triumph." She is a phenomenal person to learn from! Get a pen and notepad out and start growing!

Shay Arthur
Director, Ignite A Movement
Missionary and Itinerant Speaker
www.shayarthur.com

Sherry Chester has done what few have been able to do for me, keep me engaged in reading a book. I read it slowly, many times rereading and highlighting parts that spoke directly to me. The information that I have now adopted into my person will reflect in the way I think and act as a child of God as well as a leader of His vision. I found myself encouraged as well as inspired to commit more to God while evaluating and changing things within my control.

Ginger Maynard

Co-Founding Missionary
Servants of Hope Ministries
servantsofhope.org

Sherry is gifted in her writing ability in the way she explains the fundamental principles for living Christ-like in today's world. Her approach is straightforward and simple. It's a vision for life that is possible for each of us if only we dedicate ourselves to the daily study of His word, time alone every day between you and God, and choosing to live a life devoted to the welfare of every life surrounding us.

In today's world, many hire a life coach to help support them in the navigation of their personal and work lives. Sherry challenges us to look to God as "the best life Coach" and through the study of His word, we will find the tools, strength and courage to handle all that life brings to us. Embrace the new word she has coined as you read these pages, *VICTION*, where vision and action collide. Take this journey and travel the road to find your significance in Christ. Sherry's words teach us to anchor our *Viction* in Him and in His promise. It is there we will find the whole of who we are.

Cynthia Bayuk-Bishop
Leadership Speaks Consulting
www.leadspeak.org

I know Sherry Chester, and I know her to be someone who is maximizing the effectiveness of her assignment on this earth by fixing her eyes on Jesus. She offers a drink to the thirsty from the deep well of her life in *Viction: Where Vision and Action Collide*. She is player, coach, and cheerleader throughout this thoughtful work on living life well and avoiding the pitfalls of wasting God-given resources and time on things that don't matter. She is inviting you to go on a walk with her as she turns over every stone where secrets of insight are hidden for becoming a leader who reproduces other leaders. By following her playbook, Sherry helps you understand your life has meaning. This, in turn, makes you a person of influence for many others.

Ray Sturdivant
Founder/President of Mining the Truth
www.miningthetruth.com

Connecting Contents

Frank Foreword xvii
Pastor's Preface xxi
Inviting Introduction xxiii

Chapter 1 V - Vitals for Victionaries: Add a Helping of
   Viction Please.. 1
   What in the World is Viction?.. 1
   Valuable and Vibrant 2
   Vows Create Vacuums and Vortexes 5
   Vindication - No Place for Vanity or Vengeance................ 6
   Valiant and Virtuous, Totally in Vogue 7
   Valleys, Variables, and Victories 8
   Visibility While Being Vigilant 9
   Vessels of Versatility... 10

Chapter 2 A - Where Vision and Action Collide.................... 17
   Acknowledge, Accept, and Affirm Authority 17
   Altogether Now - Ability, Accuracy, and Accountability.. 20
   Articulately Ask for Advice, Access then Assess 23
   Advantages of Adversity and Achievement....................... 24
   Approachable, Attentive, and Authentic........................... 25
   Admirable Appreciation 27

Chapter 3 I - Inspiration is in the Identification.................. 33
   Incredibly Impressive!.. 33
   Impressions, Insecurities, and Imagination...................... 34
   Increased Inheritance 37
   Immutable Integrity 39

Inspires, Cleanses, Corrects,
  Energizes, Purifies, Strengthens 40
Innovative to be Inventive 42

Chapter 4 C - Change is the Currency 49
Calm, Cheerful Countenance 50
Called to Change and Contribute 51
Conquer Cautiousness with Credible Choices 52
Confident and Capable 53
Courageous Commitment 54
Cooperative, Considerate, and Conscientious 57
Can and Combat Cynicism - Celebrate Change 58

Chapter 5 T - Timely Transitions: Terrific, Tragic, Time-Outs, and Transformers 65
Teachable and Temperate 65
Truthful and Trustworthy 66
Terrific and Tragic 67
Thoughtful Time-outs 68
Thriving Tenacity 69
Tests within Testimonies 70
Thoughtful and Tentative 72
Titles to Track 73
Triumphant in Transitions 73

Chapter 6 I - Impeccable Individualization: Equip the People 79
Importance of Influence 79
Interactive Instruction 82
Individualize Instruction 83
Inspiring Inscriptions and Initiatives 84
Invest in Individuals 86
Instrumental Intercession 88
Impact 89

Chapter 7 O - Optimizing and Overcoming Obstacles.........95
   Optimistic Overflow... 95
   Orderly and On-Point Organization................................. 96
   Observable Opportunities.. 99
   Outstanding is Obtainable... 101
   Onward Olympian!... 102
   Open-Handed, Open-Hearted, Open-Minded 104

Chapter 8 N - Navigating Noteworthiness 111
   New, Noble, and Notable.. 111
   Networking Now.. 114
   Necessary Necessities 116
   Note the Negotiables... 117
   Navigating Noteworthiness 118

Appendix A 123
Nourishing Notes..125
Appreciative Acknowledgements..131

FRANK FOREWORD

I met Sherry Chester several years ago in the kidmin community. She has been a faithful friend and leader throughout the years we have known each other.

Sherry has the gift of encouragement amongst many other gifts. In 1 Thessalonians 5:11, we are admonished to, "encourage one another and build each other up." This is Sherry in a sentence. I always see her cheering on her team and anyone she comes in contact with. She has been a real source of encouragement to our family and our ministry.

It's now Sherry's turn to encourage you! I am super excited about this new book you are holding in your hands. God has given her the concept of *viction*, which she explains through the pages of this book.

What is viction?

Viction is the collision of vision and action. Something ministry has taught me is that the concept of vision is not enough to create change. Vision is just an idea; without a step forward, there is no destination of transformation. For example, I can envision this dream of getting my ministry, my organization, or my family to this future point, but if I do not act on this vision, I have done nothing. In the same token, action does not necessarily produce successful change. If I act with haste without proper vision, I have done nothing.

Does this concept sound familiar?

Let's refer back to James 2:14-18. Throughout this passage, God illustrates the relationship between faith and works. Faith without works is dead; works without faith is dead. To activate the two, one must collide the two. We can apply this same idea to vision and action. For success in life, I have found that vision and action go hand-in-hand, thus creating this concept of *viction*.

So, how do you combine the two?

That's an excellent question! Like I said at the beginning, I met Sherry Chester a few years ago. From the moment I met her until now, I have become a witness to her growth into becoming a powerful and bold servant of the Lord! She has been a true testament of *viction* in her life. She has challenged herself with constant learning and training, allowed room for growth, and stepped out in faith. What I love about this book is the amount of detail, life lessons, and strategic solutions that Sherry Chester has to share. From failing forward, attention to small details, and attacking life with a cheerful heart, Sherry Chester reveals some key factors to revolutionizing your life.

Because after all, don't we want to revolutionize our lives?

Of course we do! Revolutionizing our lives starts with intention. Intention is key! How do you and I intentionally change our life? How do you and I intentionally change our organization or our ministry? One thing I absolutely adore about Sherry's message and attitude going into writing this book is her absolute skill in compacting so many key messages into one readable book.

So in the end, is viction the next step for me?

If you want change, if you want direction, and if you want success, you must take the next step forward with *viction*. That's why you are reading this! The next step forward IS this book. I am so encouraged by this book and the author, my friend Sherry. As you read, remember these three points:

1. Your vision isn't enough.
2. Your actions aren't enough.
3. However, you are enough.

You are enough. A message that is often neglected. You are enough. God does not call the qualified; He qualifies the called. You don't need to be perfect. God will use you and your abilities. You are enough . . . in the beginning. You are enough to start fresh. You are enough at the starting line. However, God does not desire us to finish the race the same way we started training. From the beginning, God calls us to grow. God calls us to get from point A to point B by faith. This is where the idea of *viction* comes into play. We must learn to combine vision and action; we must rely on God to give us this *viction*.

So, if you are ready for change, you have come to the right place!

Change begins with a choice and ends in *viction*. You have completed step one by opening to page one. Prayers be to you as you start this journey!

Ryan Frank
CEO/Publisher
KidzMatter

PASTOR'S PREFACE

Stale, Stagnant, or just plain Stuck? When you see these words, they are not what we associate with our calling when we first start in our dream career or ministry. Somehow, in less than 18 months, this is the position that most leaders find themselves.

The opportunity that was fresh, new, and exciting has a similar facial expression as when you grab that bag of chips and bite into one that has been in the cabinet about a month too long. You quickly look for the nearest trash can to spit out what at one time was fresh and flavorful.

The creative river of ideas that would flow freely without a care in the world has suddenly dried up. The river of creativity that inspired world-changing ambition now smells, looks, and feels like the bayous in Louisiana; stagnant.

If we are honest and don't put a pretty bow on it, we will admit we are "just plain stuck." We are stuck without any direction, ambition, and the feeling of despair and hopelessness now begins to set in with our only thought being, "Maybe I should just quit."

What if quitting is not the answer, but there is another alternative found in the singular word *"VICTION."* Oh, you haven't heard of this? Well, get ready! Embrace it, and you'll quickly go from stale to fresh, stagnant to free-flowing, and get out of the ditch where you are stuck. *Viction* is where Vision and Action Collide. You were made for action!

Dr. Joel Tiemeyer
Founding & Lead Pastor
The Way Bible Church

INVITING INTRODUCTION

Viction is a compilation of focal points to help fine-tune areas individuals, organizations, ministries, and businesses need to expand their sphere of influence and pour into others effectively. There are particular principles timeless in life, leadership, and learning that are often overlooked and under-celebrated.[1] I have experienced both success and failure in these areas. Therefore, this is a no-judgment zone.

I write this book to you either as a friend I have already met or one I look forward to connecting with soon. You see, everyone needs a cheerleader.[2] Someone in your corner is saying, "Hey, this concept is essential for your relevancy today and your future success of tomorrow." I am here to cheer you on while you champion His call!

This work is for the specific purpose of helping individuals and organizations that keep struggling in fundamental areas and do not understand the why behind such stagnation. Much criticism is logged at churches, educational entities, and organizations by mainstream society. The reason? The very ones who should be excelling at leadership have compromised in primary areas that otherwise should be catapulting us into extreme excellence. Get ready to look at certain aspects of leadership that are, at times, less than popular to embrace, yet are the most life-changing ones.

Each chapter subheading can be read daily as a means of study, reflection, and assessment, or it can be digested a chapter at a time for insightfulness in specific areas. These writings are a reference to help gauge overall effectiveness in hearing a vision. Then utilizing action steps to know and understand our purpose, fulfilling destiny, and enjoy achievement lasting well beyond our lifetime! Collaborate with Jesus as you read. Accept His instruction and timeline. When waiting occurs, remember it intensifies the enjoyment of what comes next.

Strategic Solutions are provided at the end of each chapter to help maximize capacity. Live the life you want to have to the fullest rather than being bogged down in busyness with no end in sight. Glean from these insights so you can excel at an exponential rate.

The end of each chapter has a place to write down reflective notes in five essential areas where change is paramount for churches, educational entities, and organizations. Find the divine insights for yourself first. Then grab hold of the *victionary* ideas answering what areas you need both vision and action to move forward. Third, we are to do life together in community. What team insights do you find needful and useful? Fourth, pay attention to ideas of how to work well with young emerging leaders as there is a significant shift in the workplace. Fifth, understand the need for generational insights that affect how we authentically interact with children on a personal and engaging level.

The type of vision you cast will determine the followers you create.

Dr. Joel Tiemeyer

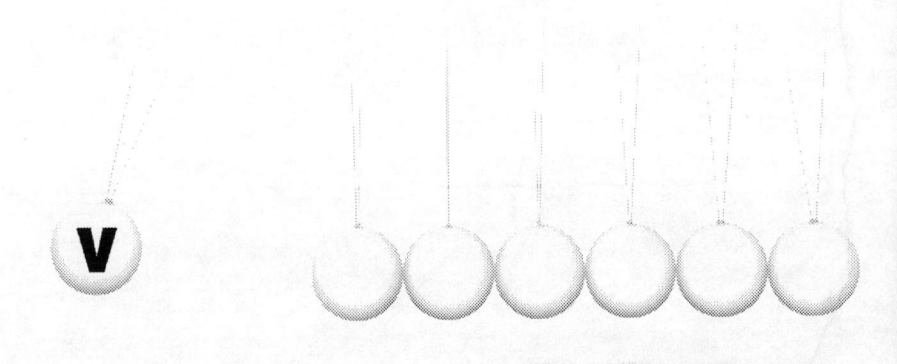

**VITALS FOR VICTIONARIES:
ADD A HELPING OF VICTION PLEASE**

CHAPTER 1

V - Vitals for Victionaries: Add a Helping of Viction Please

You've gone into my future to prepare the way, and in kindness, you follow behind me to spare me from the harm of my past. With your hand of love upon my life, you impart a blessing to me. This is just too wonderful, deep, and incomprehensible! Your understanding of me brings me wonder and strength.[1]

"Vision without action is merely a dream.
Action without vision just passes the time.
Vision with action can change the world"[2]

What in the World is Viction?

Viction is where two worlds collide intentionally. It takes more than a vision to live life to the fullest and lead well. It takes purposeful action with a specific intentionality. One without the other or in the wrong order leads to either a stalemate in life or a catastrophic series of events where picking up the rubble leads to exhaustion.

Viction is where vision and action collide to catapult your life forward with strength and tenacity. The principles outlined in each chapter go beyond traditional goals and to-do lists.

Each section in *Viction* addresses critical areas that, when left unchecked, stifles your progress and success.

It's time to embark on this journey where there is deliberate reinforcement to who you are, whose you are, and how you live. Welcome to your beautiful life unveiled where *Viction* catapults you into more significant growth and worth. Each chapter provides "Strategic Solutions" and has a reflective section entitled "Cheering You On & Championing His Call!" This space is to denote your *viction* clarification and inspiration. The five areas of focus include Divine Insight, *Victionary* Insight, Team Insight, Young Leader Insight, and Generational KidMin Insight.

Valuable and Vibrant

Valuable - In a world that places value on things more than people and "likes" on social media more than relationships, it is paramount to recognize the actual worth of people, individual team members, young leaders, and seasoned leaders. The only way to value yourself and work well with others is to know, recognize, and embrace the value of time spent alone with God at the start of each day.[3] Keep reading. Time in the secret place is better for you than a healthy breakfast or workout. This one connection breathes more vitality and creativity into you than the best of podcasts, sermons, or articles. Stop looking at the world's resources. Look to the ultimate Source.[4]

You know this, but do you make time to do this throughout the day? God created us for a relationship with Himself. He longs to talk with you. He desires to validate your significance at this very moment. Think about it. **The best life Coach ever, and Creator of the universe, wants to hang out with you continuously!** Schedule and keep these appointments. The ultimate CEO desires to meet with you; recognize the significance.

Viction: Where Vision and Action Collide

Sometimes we are not sure where to start or how to regroup with the CEO of the universe. We have canceled far too many meetings with Him or let fear and intimidation keep Him at bay. Just start, open The Bible. Devotions and books about Jesus are great. However, when you want to know someone well, you spend time with them. Start by reading the letters in red first. Ask God for understanding about everything Jesus said in Matthew, Mark, Luke, and John, the first four books in the New Testament. Spend time in the writings of Psalms and Proverbs in the Old Testament. Time together is not a speed-reading contest, nor is it cranking up Audible two times faster to complete the books. It is time to grow in relationship. I've found reading one or more chapters three times before reading further brings clarity to what God is saying and how I need to live.

For example, I camped out in Psalm 46 first thing this morning. Even though I have read this passage multiple times over the years, here's what took place while pondering 11 verses. During the first read, God highlighted His protection over me in verses 1, 7, and 11. The second time, The Father showed me, Jesus, in verse 4, as He is Living Water. The third read through, I saw His specific intent for me today. Verse 5 happens amid chaos. Here it is, *God is within her, she will not fall; God will help her at the break of day.*[5] Personalize the verse even more, and it reads like this: "God is within me, I will not fall; God will help me at the break of day." He's speaking loud and clear to you, too. Genuinely value time together now as it's an investment with high dividends and eternal value.

The litmus test is not in achievement, fame, or net worth. Significance is identity in Christ Jesus. Dismiss lies spoken over you or anyone who opposes the following:

1. God loves me, and I am loveable.[6]
2. I have the mind of Christ, and I am uniquely creative.[7]

3. I look at how to do the impossible because, with God, all things are possible.[8]

Next, look for the value in yourself and others. Since we live in a fallen "me first" world, do this. Select three people, a colleague, student, and family member. Ask God to highlight how He sees them. **Intentionally validate people based on their worth.** Remember, if you can't say something genuinely nice, don't say anything at all. Go back and ask God to give you His heart for people. You'll be glad you did. **Value God, yourself, and others.**

Vibrant – It's easy to see in a vivid photograph where the essence of an object pops at a mere glance. People are also vibrant. It's that unique WOW factor that captivates and draws people into their presence.

My most recent encounter with a vibrant child was a few weeks ago on a chilly fall, Texas morning. Keep in mind, you can be wearing shorts in the morning and need multiple layers of clothing within eight hours. Packing away seasonal clothing is risky business in the Lone Star State.

During the workweek, I greet students who are car riders at three different campuses. One particular morning, there were sleepy, timid, and clingy children. I kept waving, smiling, and opening vehicle doors. There were friendly, hugging, and wide-eyed children with many smiles and good mornings, too.

I opened yet another door, ready to speak life over the next child and their family. It's vital to remind people of all ages of their fantastic value. Before I could say a word, this cute, naturally curly-headed girl jumped out of the family vehicle and exclaimed, "I am just so excited to be here!" She kept walking briskly toward the school then energetically waving at friends arriving from an adjacent street. I wanted to stop opening doors and go to school with this girl. Surely, she had a great day. I'm relatively sure anyone who came in contact with her immediately had an extra pep in their step; I did! **Vibrant** enthusiasm exudes with ease when you know your value and the value of others.

Vows Create Vacuums and Vortexes

Have you ever seen people whose education, situation, circumstances, work ethic, or ministry looks similar to yours, and yet one is struggling significantly? At the same time, another person is soaring through life in what looks like effortless motion. Both circumstances may be factual. Underlying factors affect personal vision and the ability to act.

A vow is a promise we make ourselves that often includes the words, "always or never." A pledge of this nature is in response to a negative experience we want to protect or insulate ourselves from ever experiencing again. Inner vows are frequently made at a young age to help prevent or avoid future pain. They are usually made in the heat of a tumultuous moment and then quickly forgotten.

Vows often follow people into adulthood. It can be the reason some people quit jobs frequently or find themselves behaving like a family member they prefer not to emulate. Vows create barriers and bondages with generational effects when left unchecked. If a childhood or adult memory comes to mind where you have sworn or vowed not to act or live a particular way, then it's time to turn the tide. Since you want God-inspired vision for your life, ask Him to show you any vows that need renouncing.

Breaking inner vows might sound hard or even scary, yet the process is simple.

1. Trust God to do you good. Give Jesus free reign with your mind, will, and emotions.
2. Ask God to bring to your remembrance any vows you have made.

3. Renounce the inner vows.
4. Thank the Lord for new freedom in Jesus Christ.
5. Find an accountability partner to check up on you the next few days and weeks.

Pray - Father, thank you for doing me good. Bring to my remembrance any vows I have made and forgotten that are harmful to me (be quiet and listen). Father, I renounce _____ vow(s) I have made and replace it with your good promises for me. Thank you for revealing this to me. Show me how to walk in new freedom, in Jesus' name, Amen.

Vindication - No Place for Vanity or Vengeance

We accomplish much more when we are not concerned with who gets the credit. Remember, it's God alone who promotes.[9] Therefore, give young leaders a chance to grow. His thoughts and ways supersede our reasoning.[10] It's our responsibility to walk in integrity, whether anyone is watching or not. **It's our responsibility to follow well when we are not the lead on a project.** Pass every little test. God has plenty of resources and positions. He wants ALL of His children to shine bright.

When we seek to out-perform others in any setting or engage in office or church politics, there's a fundamental character flaw. Behind vanity is insecurity of either not looking, having, doing, or being enough. **Excessiveness in an area is a precursor for covering up personal insecurities.** Yes, we are to appear, give, do, and be our best, and that is good enough. Remember, Godliness with contentment is a significant gain.[11] **We offer our best and trust God with all the rest.**

Vanity and vengeance are evil cousins. They bring out the worst in people and seek to destroy lives. Vengeance demands its way and wants others to pay a debt they can't repay. Vengeance craves retribution and wants to punish people for wrongs they have done. Revenge and retaliation do not hurt people who have wronged you. Unforgiveness does invade and infect your body with a poison that can affect your health, wellness, and relationships. Ask God to show you anyone you need to forgive. Decide to forgive others quickly right now. Forgiveness is a great way to love yourself and others. Your emotions will line-up over time. "Vengeance is His."[12] God is trustworthy.

Valiant and Virtuous, Totally in Vogue

These are not hashtags trending on Twitter. Valiant and virtuous attributes do garner the attention of generational leaders who focus on being a part of something larger than themselves. A brave person has courage and determination in the middle of adversity. When I think of being valiant in the midst of trouble, one leader immediately comes to mind every time. This man led warriors into battle regularly, and they were successful. After one particularly hard-fought battle, the soldiers returned home to find their city burned to the ground. The people who committed this awful travesty also captured and carried away the wives and children of these 600 tired warriors.

With such grief, the men were ready to kill their leader! While devastated by significant personal loss, the organizer didn't turn to people for encouragement. The leader strengthened himself in the Lord. **Ask God for direction on any matter first.** The organizer rallied the troops. They were successful in battle and took back all their people and possessions. A great victory took place in much fatigue and exhaustion as David and his men fought bravely.[13] **Being valiant is the ability to encourage yourself when people or circumstances are not in your favor.**

Virtue abhors situational ethics and lives by a Moral Code of Conduct with high standards. Virtue remains constant even when circumstances change. There was a woman who lost her husband. Her mother-in-law and sister-in-law also became widows. Instead of staying in her hometown, Ruth follows her husband's Mother back to her country. In a foreign land, Ruth cares for Naomi even though she was relieved of the responsibility.[14] **Being virtuous is doing right when there's no personal benefit.**

Valleys, Variables, and Victories

Interwoven throughout the fabric of *viction* are valleys, variables, and victories. They frequently take place simultaneously. There are vital insights to be learned in each facet for the observant student of life and wisdom. **Valleys are the times of failing forward, learning life's lessons, and having faith when there is no emotion or feel-good moment to help push you forward.** Valley moments shape and refine character during choices to be disciplined, to do the right thing, to carry on regardless of what others think about you, the situation, or extenuating circumstances. Get close to God, die to self, and say, "If you don't do this, it cannot happen." Valleys are where lush growth takes place. Embrace the season and remember, it's not a forever place. **Refuse to dwell on things beyond your control.** Focus on controlling your thoughts and actions. Choose to be proactive rather than reactive. Celebrate every little win, for they mount up to huge victories over time. ***Victon* is often birthed in the valley as variables become gateways to unprecedented achievements.**

Variables are the countless choices presented before us daily as to how we act and react to people and circumstances. Thought patterns and habits play into this considerably. Therefore, it's essential to ask for wisdom often because He wants to give it to us in generous portions.[15] Sources "suggest that the average person makes an eye-popping 35,000 choices per day. Assuming that most people spend around seven hours per day sleeping... that makes roughly 2,000 decisions per hour or one decision every two seconds."[16] Think about it; even the number of options available to purchase a cup of coffee at Starbucks appears infinite.

Visibility While Being Vigilant

Visibility is not for the sake of yourself. Visibility is about being impactful in your sphere of influence. I heard John Bevere say this about believers, and it changed the way I view vigilance. "We are not only saved by grace to be someone; we are saved by grace to do something."[17] Being vigilant is a watchful and alert attentiveness to help others in a moment of need or to celebrate a triumph. Ask yourself, "How would Jesus help this person right now?" **Visibility improves when your eyesight comes from great insight**.

> Visibility improves when your eyesight comes from great insight.

Yesterday I sat at a newly renovated beauty shop with pieces of foil in my hair to get more low-lights and highlights. Yes, we covered the gray. While there, it became apparent several ladies around me were hurting. I laid my phone down. Remember, look up and interact with the people around you. Risky as it felt, I walked over to a younger lady and asked if I could pray for her. She just received a diagnosis rattling her world. I walked a few steps to find another dear friend facing an unexpected battle with breast cancer. We spoke words of life over her.

Meanwhile, another person is experiencing unexpected financial struggles due to the poor choices of a community member. Moments later, a single Dad and teenage son enter the shop. I engage the young teen in conversation. People of all ages need to know their importance and value. All five individuals see and experience the unconditional love of Jesus. His truths are more significant than the facts of their situations, yours, or mine. All these individuals are Christ-followers. Check your visibility. Love, encourage, and pray with others, even when there's foil in your hair.

Vessels of Versatility

This passage in 1 Corinthians 9 is the epitome of versatility. *For though I am free from all, I have made myself a servant to all, that I might win more of them... I have become all things to all people, that by all means, I might save some. I do it all for the sake of the gospel that I may share with them in its blessings.*[18]

Let's break this down together. Paul lived free of obligation to both people and things. He was secure in himself and Christ. Being versatile does not affect who I am. It offers up the availability of what I can do for others. **Being adaptable is essential. We can and must become culturally relevant while living by and adhering to the essentials of Christ-like faith.**

The Passion Translation shares verse 23 this way, "I've done all this so that I would become God's partner for the sake of the gospel." The footnote is a life lesson:

> "Paul is declaring the five motivating principles for his ministry: (1) Always start by finding common ground with those you want to reach. (2) Avoid projecting to others that you are a know-it-all. (3) Accept everyone regardless of his or her issues. (4) Be sensitive to the culture of others. (5) Use every opportunity to share the good news of Jesus Christ with people."[19]

Viction: Where Vision and Action Collide

We read these words, and our hearts exclaim, YES! **Versatility encompasses adaptability, flexibility, and changeability with right heart motives and actions.** Repeat after me, "I like change." I know what happened, you were excited to proclaim something great over your life, then you read the word. For some, it may have even looked more like letters to avoid C-H-A-N-G-E. People are often proponents of change until it affects them. **If you want to be resourceful and useful now, say "hello" to versatility and adaptability.**

Strategic Solutions

- *Viction* is where vision and action collide to catapult your life forward with tremendous strength and tenacity.
- The best life Coach ever, and Creator of the universe, wants to hang out with you continuously! Schedule and keep these appointments. This is top priority.
- Intentionally validate people based on their worth. Value God, yourself, and others.
- It's our responsibility to follow well when we are not the lead on a project.
- Excessiveness in an area is a precursor for covering up personal insecurities.
- We offer our best and trust God with all the rest.
- Ask God for direction on any matter first. Being valiant is the ability to encourage yourself when people or circumstances are not in your favor. Being virtuous is doing right when there's no personal benefit.
- Valleys are times of failing forward, learning life's lessons, and having faith when there is no emotion or feel-good moment to help push you forward.
- Refuse to dwell on those things beyond your control.
- *Viction* is often birthed in the valley as variables become gateways to unprecedented achievements.
- Visibility improves when your eyesight comes from great insight.
- Being adaptable is essential. We can and must become culturally relevant while living by and adhering to the essentials of Christ-like faith.
- Versatility encompasses adaptability, flexibility, and changeability with right heart motives and actions. Be resourceful and useful now; say "hello" to versatility and adaptability.

Viction: Where Vision and Action Collide

Cheering You On & Championing His Call!

Divine Insight
Choosing Christ & Cultivating Friendship:

_____

_____

Victionary Insight
Communicating Vision & Combining Action:

_____

_____

Team Insight
Connecting People & Creating Potential:

_____

_____

Young Leader Insight
Commending Talents & Celebrating Abilities:

_____

_____

Generational KidMin Insight
Cultivating Relationships & Collaborating Mentorships:

_____

_____

A

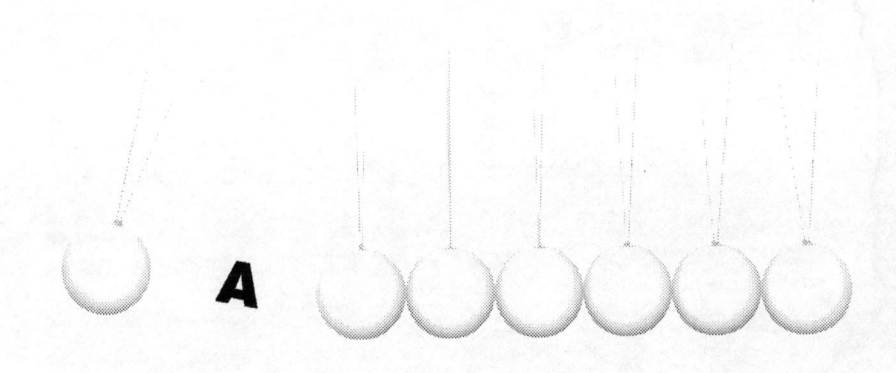

WHERE VISION AND ACTION COLLIDE

CHAPTER 2

A - Where Vision and Action Collide

*Rise up. This matter is in your hands.
We will support you, so take courage and do it.*[1]

"Authority exercised with humility, and obedience accepted with delight are the very lines along which our spirits live." – C.S. Lewis.[2]

Acknowledge, Accept, and Affirm Authority

In the absence of these three "A"s, growth as a visionary, whether in the boardroom, classroom, or mailroom, is severely limited. Respect for authority promotes a long life. If you desire to be "the boss" or already are one, do a checkup. Everyone is answerable to someone. We are ultimately accountable to God. Respect for authority is fundamental to your future success. You can know all the right people and have a great plan; without recognizing and submitting to authority, you are dead in the water, my friend.

At times we have become skeptical of people who have misbehaved. Government entities, the institution of marriage, and family dynamics have been abused and misused. Yet, places of authority command respect, for it's God who promotes.[3] Therefore, it's vitally important to follow God, the ultimate Leader, and authority figure.[4]

Accept Family First - The first commandment with

the promise of a long life instructs us to give honor to Father and Mother.[5] Society has devalued these roles significantly. Television has made a mockery of man's wisdom by portraying them as stupid and indecisive in many sitcoms and commercials. The media has made the external appearance of a woman and her career far more important than her character or her role as wife or mother. Advertisers target children who dictate many of the purchasing decisions about where to eat and what movies to watch. The bigger is better mentality has families chasing after things that cannot satisfy.

When wrong looks right and right looks wrong, there is a terrible problem of pandemic proportions.[6] The enemy has actively sought to undermine the family unit. Christians have quietly and passively allowed this to happen through an ever-increasing large box in one or more rooms in our homes. Even in very remote areas on other continents where there are tents or shelters with sand floors, televisions can be heard and seen. I'm not against owning a TV or watching one in moderation. As with all things, wisdom, guidelines, and self-control are necessary.

Whether your parents are living or deceased, giving recognition is not contingent upon their good behavior, lifestyle, or accomplishments. Honor is God-ordained instruction for recognizing that even though people are imperfect, respect is due to those who give life and help raise you. There are situations where relationships are less than perfect and strained. Being bitter and holding onto unforgiveness does nothing but hurt everyone involved. Ultimately it hurts your current and future relationships when past mistakes repeat themselves. Forgiveness does not release a parent from their accountability or responsibility. It does give you much favor with God and man. **Mercy and grace abound where forgiveness is found.**

Most people live in a post "Leave it to Beaver" family. My parents divorced when I was six. I saw my Dad, who left us and the ministry, very little before he passed away. We did reconcile before he became ill after a thirty-year gap. I initiated the visit after encouragement from Maxie, my husband, and friends in our homegroup. I understand pain and rejection.

I wish family brokenness ended there. I have been married twice. The first marriage ended in divorce. I finished raising our four daughters as a single parent and desire a redo for multiple moments during this season.

Years later, I remarried a trusting man and embarked on a blended family where his young adult children lost their mother unexpectedly due to a massive heart attack. I became Gi Gi to his young grandchildren. We did our best to make things right from mistakes we both experienced earlier in life. Marvelous Maxie passed away in March 2019. Things changed in ways I couldn't foresee.

I have learned much and forgiven much. Considerable time and energy go into earning trust and restoration of relationships. **As far as it depends on you, find the good and acknowledge positive traits where you can, how you can, and when you can safely.** Repent for the times you deemed it acceptable to make a mockery and speak ill of parental figures whether they are absent or present, a success or a failure in your life. Plant new seeds and declare God's promises; your legacy will thank you in years to come.

Affirm Authority - Family leaders, church leaders, community leaders, and political leaders are due respect in direct response to scripture. Romans 13:1 says, *Let everyone be subject to the governing authorities, for there is no authority except that which God has established. God has established the authorities that exist.*[7]

We honor those in leadership because they are the authorities God put in place.[8]

Social media makes it easy to be hypercritical of anyone who thinks differently. The problem is far more systemic than political parties. Resist the temptation to speak ill of others. A word to the wise, pray for someone the length of time you desire to vent. Accomplish much more on bended knee.

Even when authority is used correctly, it can still be unsettling. Human nature prefers to rule self because we think we can do it better, so did Adam and Eve. These thoughts are rooted in selfish ambition and vain conceit, better known as pride.

If submitting to family and or authority are areas where you struggle, let's stop right now and break off a spirit of rebellion. Personal growth is stifled where rebellion resides.

1. Repent of negative words spoken against anyone in authority.[9] There's excellent healing in this for you and gracious relief to others.
2. Choose to think well of parents and those in power locally, nationally, and internationally. **Thoughts proceed words, check your thinking.**
3. Pray daily for those in authority (family, business, church, and government leaders).[10] **Being prayerless is careless and powerless.**
4. Speak well of authority. Show respect to those who have been anointed, appointed, selected, or elected.
5. Be purposeful in thanking and showing appreciation to those in authority.

Altogether Now - Ability, Accuracy, and Accountability

Ability - Recognize and cultivate your strengths. Your productivity and motivation will soar when you focus on your giftings rather than your weaknesses. Next, surround yourself with people who have abilities in the areas that are not your strengths. Quite frankly, I'm not good at gardening or landscaping. I have an appreciation of fresh vegetables and flowers, yet not one green thumb. A local garden stand and perennials are my friends. We cannot do everything well. You are unique with a purpose only you can fulfill. Cultivate the dreams and vision within.

Respectfully embrace the capable qualities of others. Their younger or older expertise does not belittle your strengths. The truth is, we are better together. Notice the word is respect, not compare. Comparison is wicked and robs you of joy; back away from it now. Comparison has a sneaky cousin named competition; both seek to deter you from greatness.

If you are naturally competitive, make the competition about becoming the best version of yourself. Learn from others while remembering the plumb line of excellence is within The Word. We have an audience of One to please. When you have God's approval, nothing else really matters. He is the Standard. Utilizing abilities is as imperative as the accuracy of doing things well.

Accuracy - The Gallup Poll recently reported shocking results about the workplace.[11] Seventy percent of employees disengage at work. Mediocrity has plummeted workers to an all-time low. Yet we are governed by an all-time high, *Therefore whoever relaxes one of the least of these commandments and teaches others to do the same will be called least in the kingdom of heaven, but whoever does them and teaches them will be called great in the kingdom of heaven.*[12]

People who detach from work find it easier to manipulate content to show what people want to hear. Skewed data is a risky business for any team and far from honoring. Remember, *You must have accurate and honest weights and measures, so that you may live long in the land the Lord your God is giving you.*[13] Be gripped by what stirs the heart of God. Then be honest with yourself and others. Time, money, and resources are limited. The word "limit" is not harmful; it merely determines boundaries for any given season. **Acknowledge and speak**

the truth about where you are today. Then real growth can happen in new ways.

Accountability at Work - Although attendance is indicative of a thriving children's department, church, or organization; responsibility demands more. With generational ministry, there are a plethora of ways to teach, creative ways to thematically decorate, and innovative ways to host events. If these activities aren't producing growth, salvation, discipleship, and additional opportunities to reach people, something has gone awry.

Determine ways to measure tangible results and specific outcomes. Knowing **"Who does what by when?" should be a part of daily assessments.**[14] Use an Impact Chart to track growth while holding yourself and the team accountable. Remember, *All Scripture is breathed out by God and profitable for teaching, for reproof, for correction, and for training in righteousness.*[15]

Accountability that's Personal - One phrase I frequently say, "Measure what you treasure." You are the treasure in an earthly vessel.[16] Make sure you have an accountability partner who is a spiritually mature Christ-follower stewarding their life well. Select a mentor who is somewhat removed from your daily circumstances as they can speak more objectively into your life. Mentors may change with seasons of life. Yet I consistently visit them weekly or bi-weekly.

There are also mentors I have not met yet. They shape my life through their books, YouTube channels, and podcasts. Pay attention to those whose words resonate and energize you. Then, study those who aggressively advance the kingdom of God. There's much to be learned from forerunners.

Viction: Where Vision and Action Collide

Articulately Ask for Advice, Access then Assess

Make "The Ask" - *You don't have because you don't ask.*[17] When there's something you want to learn more about, be specific in the inquiry. Fear and doubt keep many people from making "an ask" that can have valuable results.

I'd been in education as a Central Office Administrator for 21 years when God started doing something new. Leaving seemed unthinkable. It was the decision of a lifetime. **Big decisions call for significant confirmations.** During this time, I read a book entitled *Purpose, Destiny, and Achievement*. I noticed the author's international ministry is in Franklin, Tennessee. We would be flying to the area shortly to see the youngest daughter graduate from nursing school. I emailed Dr. William Greenman to express appreciation for his book. Then I asked if Maxie and I could treat him and his wife to lunch while in the area. He responded within hours with a resounding, yes!

Seek Access - The luncheon allowed asking how to make significant transitions well. Dr. Greenman willingly shared remarkable insights. He was surprised I asked for the meeting. I was astonished at how few people were not beating his door down as the textbook was relevant and life changing. Gain wisdom by asking for advice from those who know more than you. Others are willing to share. **Be teachable, be moldable, and make the request for access.**

Assess What You Learn - The meeting with the Greenmans was fantastic as Maxie, and I left encouraged. With any new content comes pertinent questions.

1. Does what I learned line up with scripture?
2. Is the information applicable for me individually?
3. If, when, and how should this new wisdom be implemented?

Gaining fresh insight is terrific, yet there is a caution light here. In getting together, especially in a conference, workshop, or webinar setting, we hear fabulous ideas that work well for someone else. There's an innate desire to replicate their success model immediately. In most cases, this doesn't work well. Listen to new material presented in light of your vision and mandate from God. Every good idea is not necessarily the best idea for you individually, the team collectively, or the church and organization holistically. Know the DNA of your ministry. **Determine when and how new content and ideas will take place as planning and timing are essential for success.**

Advantages of Adversity and Achievement

Vision and action collide on the hills of both adversity and achievement. Many believers prefer not to hear that difficulty promotes the gospel. It was verifiable in the early days of the church.[18] It is also the case with underground churches on other continents.[19]

Adversity - Trials are the impetus for growth even when family, friends, in-laws, co-workers, or church members come against you for what feels like no apparent reason.[20] Adversity is the refiner's fire. It causes impurities that are not Christ-like to rise to the top. We give Him the muck; our reflective likeness becomes more apparent. Remember, Jesus is coming back for a Bride, The Church, who is without spot or blemish. We should no longer be surprised by friendly fire or the undermining of The Bible and Freedom of Religion as we know it in America.

"Gird up your loins." Now is the time we advance the kingdom of God with tenacity by how we teach children and reach out to their immediate and extended families. Set the coloring sheets down and recognize there is no junior Holy Spirit. Children are thirsty for The Truth and real power. Otherwise, they turn to the counterfeit skills of Harry Potter and Dora because the church is not walking in power and authority. Change your mindset. Adversity helps us run and finish the race well. Adversity banishes mediocrity. Do the right thing lest you settle for far less than God's best. Be brave, be bold, for the Lord our God is with you!

Advantages of Achievement - The flip side of the coin to adversity is achievement. No one season lasts forever. Accomplishments help us celebrate wins along the way. Successes provide wind under our sails to help us embrace lessons learned. Achievements place perseverance in the right perspective. Successes validate the good in others while seeing how God is moving in us.[21] Acknowledge wins along the way; be thankful.[22] Take time to observe victories in specific areas:

1. **Praise People** in ways they can see, hear and appreciate.
2. **Emphasize Core Values** as favorable reinforcement.
3. **Recognize Lessons Learned** by sharing specific examples.
4. **Highlight Measurable Outcomes** that exceed expectations.
5. **Celebrate Growth** on-purpose in proportion to the win.

Approachable, Attentive, and Authentic

Approachable - When people perceive us to be too busy, we are no longer accessible and have not learned to manage time well. When people start with, "I hate to bother you because you are so busy", it's time to see what consumes our busyness. Leaders who wear "busy" like a badge are typically ineffective leaders.

Are we living project-oriented or people-oriented? I am goal, performance, and outcome-driven. Yet if I have finished a project at the expense of snubbing a person, I left the very character of Jesus in the workroom, meeting room, classroom, boardroom, laptop, or desktop. Unfortunately, I have been guilty of leaving His attributes in every one of these locations because I didn't allow and schedule enough time for what He deems most important, people. Strip the badge of "busyness" off your chest right now. Stomp it into the ground quickly and ask God to give you a heart for people. We will spend eternity with people, not paper, programs, projects, or initiatives. Focus on what matters most.

Attentive - Being attentive is listening to others and making eye contact without thinking of your next statement. Be engaged at the moment. Refrain from multitasking; it's a distraction and turn-off. Set time limits to move things along or defer to someone else who might provide more assistance than you can. Stay in the moment; you will be more engaging and productive.

> Have enough passion for Jesus that you have compassion for others.

Jesus taught crowds of people. He stopped to interact with the one and so we must do the same. Children's ministries, churches, organizations, businesses, and schools have the same customer base; people. When in Pemba, Africa, three years ago, I heard Heidi Baker repeatedly say, "stop for the one." **Have enough passion for Jesus that you have compassion for others.** Children and families will want to hear what you have to say when you build a relationship first. See the faces, get to know the individual's story, then hunger to see if they know Jesus.

Authentic - I helped with a Recovery Group at a local church over a decade ago. One particular Friday night, people were excited to see one another and cutting up loudly. A man by the name of Mark stepped up to the microphone and started speaking with a distinctively East Texas drawl.

Mark shared about going into a prison where they allowed him access to the solitary confinement area. He got down on bended knee and crawled from door to door. With his nose pressed to the ground, Mark asked one question at every cell even though he could not see the prisoners' faces. He asked, "Do you know Jesus?" He listened and responded. This question was his interaction with anyone he met wherever he went. Mark was genuinely authentic with people, and they responded accordingly. Mark died prematurely. His funeral was a testament that he ultimately focused on what matters most. I had already led individuals to Jesus and discipled people of all ages before that night. Yet hearing his question and story forever changed how I would reach out to people. If this has raised questions in your heart or mind, please go to Appendix A this very moment as I ask, "Do You Know Jesus?"

Admirable Appreciation

Praise spoken in excess is nauseating. Therefore, be kind, specific, and validating when giving appreciation to people. Sincerity and specificity are like a breath of fresh air. When we focus on the good, the negative dissipates.

Be specific when being thankful. It's the difference between saying, "Thanks for helping" versus "Thanks for getting here early to turn on the computers and set out the iPads. You make mornings an excellent experience for everyone who walks through our doors." Appreciation supports validation. Make this a priority when communicating with people.

Strategic Solutions

- Mercy and grace abound, where forgiveness is found.
- As far as it depends on you, find the good and acknowledge positive traits where you can, how you can, and when you can safely.
- Thoughts proceed words, check your thinking.
- Being prayerless is careless and powerless.
- Acknowledge and speak the truth about where you are today. Then real growth can happen in new ways.
- Respectfully embrace the capable qualities of others.
- "Who does what by when?" should be a part of daily assessments.
- Measure what you treasure.
- Make sure you have an accountability partner who is a spiritually mature Christ-follower stewarding their life well.
- Big decisions call for significant confirmations.
- Be teachable, be moldable, and make "the ask" for access.
- Determine when and how new content and ideas are presented, as planning and timing are essential for success.
- Set the coloring sheets down and recognize there is no junior Holy Spirit. Children are thirsty for The Truth and real power.
- Have enough passion for Jesus that you have compassion for others.

Viction: Where Vision and Action Collide

Cheering You On & Championing His Call!

Divine Insight
Choosing Christ & Cultivating Friendship:

_____

_____

Victionary Insight
Communicating Vision & Combining Action:

_____

_____

Team Insight
Connecting People & Creating Potential:

_____

_____

Young Leader Insight
Commending Talents & Celebrating Abilities:

_____

_____

Generational KidMin Insight
Cultivating Relationships & Collaborating Mentorships:

_____

_____

INSPIRATION IS IN THE IDENTIFICATION

CHAPTER 3

I - Inspiration is in the Identification

You did not choose me, but I chose you and appointed you that you should go and bear fruit and that your fruit should abide, so that whatever you ask the Father in my name, he may give it to you.[1]

"In life, it's not what you think you are that holds you back, it's what you think you are not."[2]

Incredibly Impressive!

God is impressed with you, His distinctive creation. Study and celebrate the unique differences in you. **Your difference determines destination.** Recognizing your value catapults you into your destiny. Be you! Your uniqueness helps you appreciate the exceptionality in others. You were born to lead and leverage ideas.

The greatest gift you can offer God, yourself and others is undertaking endeavors that bring you much joy. Refuse to perceive this as self-serving. A focused life of intentional action creates synergy for stronger movement. If you delight in seeing kids have "AHA" experiential moments, then be relentless in this place and space. Change the world one child, class, city, country, and continent at a time. The dream in your heart is the passion you pursue. You were born for more!

Consider Genesis 6:8, *But Noah was a pleasure to the*

Lord.³ Did your heart leap? It should have. God views you the same way. Another version of The Bible reads this way, *Noah found favor with the Lord.*⁴ Others state, *Noah found grace in the eyes of the Lord.*⁵ The Contemporary English Version (CEV) shares the verse in another clear manner, *The Lord was pleased with Noah.* Responsiveness to God compounds favor, creativity, and innovation because God takes pleasure in you, precious one.

Let me remind you what makes you impressive and why you can lead a world that is starving for authentic leadership. You have the ability and courage to inspire others to greatness while staying faithful to your call. You are capable of taking an idea and turning it into a workable concept for the greater good because you are fearless.

Impressions, Insecurities, and Imagination

Impressions - There are mind impressions, first impressions, and lasting impressions. Like a two-faced coin, each either add or subtract value.

Mind Impressions - The idea in your mind's eye sees yourself as either increasing or decreasing. You treat yourself with contempt or respect. **You are eating and digesting what your mouth is speaking.**⁶ Your mind is continuously making an imprint of whom your heart says you are. Have brave conversations with yourself to where the mind impressions match God's remarkable thoughts of you.

First Impressions - Mike Murdock shares two things about order that I find incredibly applicable to first and lasting impressions. First impressions, "little hinges swing big doors."⁷ One divine connection can move mountains in minutes where you have spent years trying to make something happen. Connectivity happens through impressions, thereby cultivating relationships. **Your presentation, stature, and character**

are the business card of Jesus, both personable and stunning. Express Him skillfully and effectively.

Lasting Impressions - These happen in a matter of moments when you take the focus off yourself and add value to others. Listen attentively to people and gain insight. Engage by asking thoughtful questions. Find out what energizes them, including how you can help. Remember their story and share a concise, transparent story about yourself. Then do what my Momma told me, smile, and look people in the eye.

Every word spoken and action made is either erecting barricades to stop vision or constructing connections where engagement flourishes. *Viction* is the imprint you leave on the hearts and minds of others. **People want to follow someone who has seen the prize and has a clear-cut way of getting there.** "You can get anywhere you want to go if you are willing to take enough small steps."[8] People are desperate for genuine leaders where information saturation is dominant, and the application is waning.

Internal Insecurities - "Insecurity rests from the way we have coped rather than [been healed]."[9] Apprehension, self-doubt, timidity, and change can leave us vulnerable when we give way to such thoughts. Reject their ability to define you and send them packing! Dismiss internal self-sabotage and fulfill your destiny.

The apostle Paul had many regrets he could have focused on regarding who he murdered and the treatment of other believers before he became a Christ-follower. However, He chose to forget those things in the past and press forward.[10] So, what, you messed up. Every person before you and those after you will do the same. Learn and grow from prior insecurities and poor choices.

External Insecurities - Critical people are unhappy with themselves, or they are angry that you dare to do something outside the norm. When people behave in a way you don't understand, assess the situation, see what part you have played in the interaction and make the necessary adjustments. With the biggest air hug I can give you right now, let me say this. "Get over what others think about you." Lay down introspection and fear of people's opinions. Then greet the next person you meet and seek how to love and serve them well at that moment.

Imagination - The negative side of the imagination is thoughts that seek to exalt themselves against God. "What ifs" inside your good-looking head are counter-productive and seek to polarize even the most remarkable of opportunities. When left to run wild negatively, the imagination will borrow unrealized trouble to thwart even the most basic productivity. Buyer beware; don't take what the enemy is peddling.

An upside to the imagination is fathoming every good and excellent thing that happens when maximizing aspirations, potential, and resources. The mind is where problems are solved, memory improves, curiosity is piqued, and self-confidence develops. If you can see it and believe it, then indeed, you can achieve it, for the very same Spirit that raised Christ from the dead dwells in you. How will you wield your sword? Will you tear yourself to smithereens with what-ifs and foreboding thoughts? Or will you preemptively determine to imagine the greatest and hope for the best? Live with unsurpassed resolve to dream big and lead with clarity.

Icky "I"s: Inferiority, Iniquity, and Infirmity

Familiar with the saying, "The ayes have it?" The phrase is said when those who vote in favor of something win. The enemy seeks to make us think he has won with his ploys and antics. Here are three primary tactics he uses to wage war on our minds.

Inferiority - Thoughts of inadequacy can make you think you are an imposter and inept at making correct decisions and carrying out the purposes and

> Both success and failure can be traced to whatever you think and do daily.

plans of God for your life. The enemy wants to make you think you are less than sufficient at every turn. **Stop obsessing about your flaws when God is blessing you for a particular cause to where He gets all the applause.** The enemy's attempts don't work when you think and speak about your identity in Christ. He'll switch to a different tactic when necessary.

Iniquity - One of Satan's favorite things to do is remind you about stuff you've done wrong. He wants you dwelling on your mistakes rather than triumphs. **Both success and failure can be traced to whatever you think and do daily.** Remember, he's referred to as the "accuser of the brethren" for a reason.[11] When you repent quickly of sin and keep an attitude of gratitude, the deceiver will seek to distract you differently.

Infirmity - It starts with a little annoyance of pain here or there. He will offer us a cold or flu to see if we will take the bait. One way or the other, his sole purpose is to cause you to be ineffective. He hates it when you and I walk in our authority that by Jesus' stripes, we're healed. Recognizing and countering these tactics breaks the enemy's power over your thought life. Spoil the identity theft plan by remembering who made you, saved you, and healed you.

Increased Inheritance

Increased inheritance involves being super practical as much as it does being mega brave. It happens ... *precept upon precept; line upon line, here a little and there a little.*[12] Daily spiritual and physical decisions happen with sustained vision and action, AKA *Viction*. Every hour counts, and every day matters for new levels of elevation. Pour into others in small ways daily. Fill their cup, and yours begins to overflow. Helping others succeed is living a life of legacy sowing favor into your own life as well.[13]

Going Way Beyond - Chastity Marie is a friend who says she could have voted herself most unlikely to succeed. She experienced trauma in her childhood, yet coped by imagining herself someplace else. Her delivery date with her second child was the day after her high school graduation. Amid much adversity, she always saw herself destined for greatness, yet didn't know how it would come about.

Chastity's accomplishments in sales put her at the pinnacle of a successful career, yet she needed a change. With knees knocking, Chastity changed jobs and began working in LeVel, a health and wellness multi-level marketing company. She trusted God with every aspect of the transition because "He is crazy sufficient." She works diligently and empowers others. Part of her current inheritance is earning a seven-digit figure income. During her success, Chastity shared with me "that inheritance is not about her life's success rather her life's significance." The ***messy bun millionaire***, her Facebook and Instagram tag, asks several questions of herself and others when discussing inheritance and success. She asked the first four questions faster than I could type.

1. What talents and gifts are on the inside of you?
2. What do you need to walk and live out your talents?
3. What does the best version of yourself look like?
4. What sets your heart on fire and elevates your heart rate?

Afterwards she leaned in and asked the fifth question with deliberate poise and tenacity. "**Are you willing to love people for a living?**" The pinnacle of servant leadership rests in this one stunning question. Jesus is the most excellent leader of all time. What does He do repeatedly? He loves unconditionally. Perhaps the focus has been on lesser things far too long.

I asked Chasity, who leads thousands, to share her "Daily Dos," She has multiple non-negotiables. Get ready:

- Don't use a cell phone as an alarm; it's a distraction.
- Move; elevate your heart rate.
- Have an attitude of gratitude.
- Master your miracle morning; start it well with God.
- Stay in the seat of learning at all times.
- Position yourself to be with those who are doing more and learning more.
- Embrace mentors.

The direct questions and the daily do list reinforce this. **True leaders are rooted in humility and teachability**. Great leaders desire something better for others and repeatedly reflect credit to God and their team or tribe. For more information about this phenomenal leader, see the End Notes.[14]

Immutable Integrity

Integrity is described with words like creditability, honesty, or being trustworthy. It reflects an individual who can keep a confidence. In *The Speed of Trust*, Stephen M. R. Covey defines integrity as "a person who has no gap between intent and behavior... when he or she is whole, seamless, the same, inside and out."[15] He refers to this as congruence, where they walk their talk and remain faithful to a core set of values.[16]

Integrity is the premise or baseline of a person's core beliefs. Otherwise, a person readily resorts to "the ends justifies the means" mentality. Situational ethics readily evade integrity. It's why people, workplaces, and ministries crumble when they resort to deceit, manipulation, and scandal to maintain a façade.

Integrity far supersedes ethics. Let's compare the difference. During years of working with federal programs, audits were the norm. Compliance visits sought to determine if the program and people responsible for implementation were following the rules and regulations. Compliance is about the rules, and the end justifying the means. Integrity is about consistency across the board based on honesty, truth, and right living.

A familiar story comes to mind where a child has to sit in a corner and looks obedient until stating. "I'm sitting on the outside but standing on the inside." The same is true of people who look busy in the workplace yet are surfing the Internet for the latest in sports or home goods. The defiant examples don't reflect aspects of integrity.

Training to equip generational leaders must focus on core values and how these values translate to specific acceptable consistent behaviors. The world is desperate to see genuine accountability, believability, and credibility in the Body of Christ. Reading and listening to scripture solves integrity issues at an accelerated rate because you are chasing after the very heart of God regarding the situation and circumstances set before you. Ascertain and embrace what The Word does for you daily as you read, listen, and speak it forth with great boldness and clarity. The Living Word:

Inspires, Cleanses, Corrects, Energizes, Purifies, Strengthens

There is a direct correlation between hearing the voice of God and illumination for daily living. Devour the Word of God with aggressive assertiveness. Refuse to look to people first. The Bible and prayer will solve a host of problems for yourself and those around you. **People cannot think themselves into right doing and living; it's based on believing and acting on the word of God.** Integrity is a heart matter and seems allusive to many believers since the ways of the world have infiltrated the church, marketplace, and all types of educational systems.

Listed below are key words to help clarify what living a life of immutable integrity looks like. Notice how the words interconnect. Missing one or more of these traits leaves a massive void in life and leadership. The best leadership advice on the market is not how to finish projects faster or how to get people to listen to you better. The best practical pointers on leadership are the ones that help more fully develop integrity. Other facets of leadership will come quickly when core building blocks are in place.

Accountability - "God won't hold us accountable for what we could not do, but He will hold us accountable for the things we could have done."[17] God's approval matters more than anything else.

Believability - People are thirsty to have someone in their life who is authentic. Being consistently persistent in what we think, do, and say points others to the Christ-like way. Believability and trust go hand in hand.

Credibility - Walk away from those who speak negatively about people or circumstances.[18] Toxic individuals undermine authority figures to gain control. What we hear has a direct influence over what we speak. Credibility comes from doing what is right and speaking the truth in love.

Dependability - When you commit to doing something, follow through. Even when it costs you additional time, resources, or the task becomes more challenging to complete than expected. Better to complete a few projects with excellence than to do multiple tasks in mediocrity that have to be redone by you or others numerous times. Dependability increases your accountability, believability, and credibility.

Equitability - Treat each individual and circumstance the same. Be fair, consistent, and impartial. Being equitable with people and in life is being honest, unbiased, above board, and on the up and up. Equity makes no room for bias or prejudice.

Predictability - There is safety when people know what to expect from your behavior and actions. Provide a consistent baseline to where your emotions are in check, and responses are fair and impartial.

Reliability - Closely tied to believability and credibility, reliability brings to the table a quality of performance that is steadfast and loyal. There's a consistency that's reputable, safe, and constant.

Stability - Balanced, rational, and trustworthy behavior is essential for creativity to occur. A stable person, organization, and ministry can move forward even when a crisis arises because the durability of stability is a tremendous safety net.

Speak-ability - Much emphasis rests on the ability to articulate and communicate. Integrity says the "who, speak, and do" are to be congruent and match up really well. There are many phenomenal speakers and teachers. Upon closer observation what they say and how they behave cause many to walk away.

Workability - It's simple to say yet seen less nowadays. Work is exerting mental or physical energy to achieve or complete a specific result or purpose.

Some of the best leaders in life have no formal title. When they are given a title it rarely reflects the depth of diversity or what they can bring to the table. Watch and listen, genuine integrity can be very quiet and unassuming. As with wisdom, it can be seen and drawn out of others when seeking to learn.

Innovative to be Inventive

Inventive innovation is about being imaginative, ingenious, and resourceful. Creativity designs something original, breaks new ground, develops unique thoughts, and utilizes God-given talents and gifts. God has been doing this through the ages, as seen in Proverbs 22:29, *Do you see someone skilled in their work? They will serve before kings; they will not serve before officials of low rank.*

Viction: Where Vision and Action Collide

Sitting in a high school senior English class, I never thought life would take me in the direction of writing. Yet years later, professional responsibilities involved grant writing. I will not geek-out here and share crazy experiences of implementing programs. I do want to share how personally developing this one skill set opened doors.

The district submitted and received a state-level Laura Bush Family Literacy Grant. We could send a representative to meet the First Lady of Texas. I sent a colleague who would be implementing the grant. A few years later, there was an opportunity to seek a federal Barbara Bush Family Literacy grant. Less than a dozen grants were awarded throughout the nation that year. As a recipient of the award, there was an invitation for two of us to attend a reception at the White House hosted by First Lady Laura Bush. This God-given talent of grant writing made way for me to meet multiple people of significant influence. The reception was special as God had divine appointments with her and others I will forever cherish.

Being innovative seeks to know where opportunity exists, how it can be done and the way something can and needs to be delivered. Innovation is about growing beyond the limits of your comfort zone. In Daniel 6:3 it's referred to as an excellent or extraordinary spirit, *Then this Daniel began distinguishing himself among the commissioners and satraps because he possessed an extraordinary spirit, and the king planned to appoint him over the entire kingdom.* You, too, possess a most excellent spirit and extraordinary qualities. Create an innovative solution through the doors of a pure heart, the clarity of purposeful thinking, and *viction* of transparent eyes.

Strategic Solutions

- Your difference determines destination.
- You are eating and digesting what your mouth is speaking.
- Your presentation, stature, and character are the business card of Jesus, both personable and stunning. Express Him skillfully and effectively.
- People want to follow someone who has seen the prize and has a clear-cut way of getting there.
- Stop obsessing about your flaws when God is blessing you for a particular cause to where He gets all the applause.
- Both success and failure can be traced to whatever you think and do daily.
- True leaders are rooted in humility and teachability.
- Training to equip generational leaders must focus on core values and how these values translate to specific acceptable consistent behaviors.
- People cannot think themselves into right doing and living; it's based on believing and acting on the word of God.

Viction: Where Vision and Action Collide

Cheering You On & Championing His Call!

Divine Insight
Choosing Christ & Captivating Friendship:

_____

_____

Victionary Insight
Communicating Vision & Combining Action:

_____

_____

Team Insight
Connecting People & Creating Potential:

_____

_____

Young Leader Insight
Commending Talents & Celebrating Abilities:

_____

_____

Generational KidMin Insight
Mentorships:

_____

_____

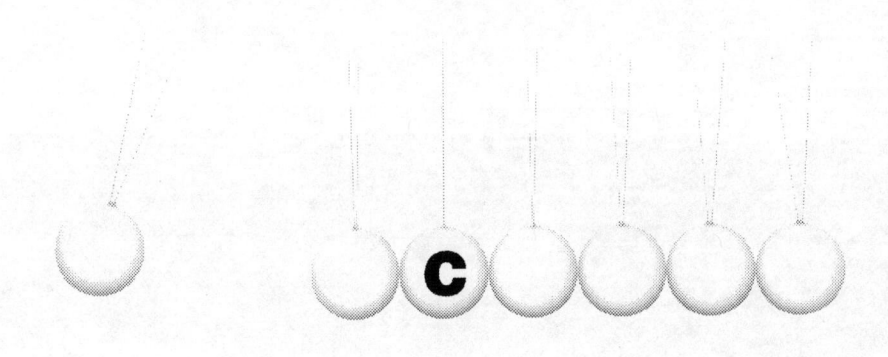

CHANGE IS THE CURRENCY

CHAPTER 4

C - Change is the Currency

See, I am doing a new thing! Now it springs up; do you not perceive it? I am making a way in the wilderness and streams in the wasteland.[1]

"Beloved don't forget that every day must be a day of advancement. If you have not made advancement since yesterday, in a measure, you are a backslider. There is only one way for you between Calvary and glory, and it is forward. It is every day forward. It is no day back. It is advancement with God. It is cooperation with Him in the Spirit."[2]

More than words, I seek to add meaningful value to areas where change challenges us the most. Change is the new currency in which the world revolves. The earth is more chaotic and tumultuous than ever before. The masses are desperate for individuals to emerge who will bring about *viction*. Remember, *viction* is both the foresight of a solid course of action coupled with tangible steps to offer something better than people have experienced.

Interestingly enough, those crying out for improvement are the ones who fight forward movement at every turn due to fear of the unknown and insecurities. Like young David, when he slew the giant Goliath, we too must focus on how big our God is rather than the size of change.

Calm, Cheerful Countenance

Calm - It's easy to be calm when everything is going our way. Life is more comfortable when there are no encroaching deadlines, bills are paid, and life is good. *(Make sure to thank God for these blessings.)* Being calm is staying relaxed when external situations aren't ideal. Composure refines us through tests of acceleration, crisis, conflict, decline, stagnation, or growth. Tangible stressors provide opportunities for the calm strength of God to guard our hearts.[3] Even when writing, I found myself reflective about the vulnerability that occurs when being transparent. Then I heard God gladly share.

I call you friend,
> *for as you trust in me, therein you can depend.*

You are to help people ever be on the mend,
> *even when you think you're at your wit's end.*

Continue to extend your helping hand and lend.
> *I promise it's not a dead end.*

The lengths you go to amend is the very heart I commend.
> *It is you I send, knowing change helps everyone comprehend.*

Countenance - The word countenance is used 52 times in the Bible, either when someone walks away from God in disobedience or when describing the emotions of people who are sad, discouraged, angry, or afraid. Change can evoke these responses when uncertainty is encroaching. In other instances, countenance refers to the hope we have in God. The examples of countenance are varied, yet we can readily see another person's look, and they can perceive ours.

Choose to Be Cheerful in the Midst of Change - Recognize I'm not talking about some fake, sappy type of happiness. Countenance defines demeanor. As an emoji reflects feelings, your appearance is a barometer of Christlikeness. The reliability in change is this. *Those who* *look to Him are radiant; their faces are never covered with shame.*[4] **Change is profound, where a calm, cheerful countenance abounds.**

Called to Change and Contribute

Learning to lead change is one of the most proactive measures leaders can take in ministry, education, organization, or business. Leading change is purposefully intentional and, at times, defies current success to take hold of more significant future victories. Here are some clear pathways to help lead change.

1. **Create Urgency** - Clearly define why the change is necessary.
2. **Communicate Vision** - Make it understandable and easy to restate.
3. **Capture Buy-In** - Seek consensus whenever and wherever possible.
4. **Champion Change** - Carry out transitions with repeated consistency.
5. **Celebrate Wins** - Identify wins early and celebrate with people often.

Conquer the past by focusing on the future. Strategize, prioritize, organize, and revolutionize. **Recognize those who lead change are required to have a great depth of character.**

1. **Conscientious in Creating Urgency** - Explain that the pain of staying stagnant is far more harmful than the pain associated with change. Be honest and diligent in addressing the truth surrounding the transition.

2. **Conviction to Communicate Vision** - Hear a leader's heart, then it can be followed. Paint a compelling picture of the future.
3. **Ceaseless about Capturing Buy-In** - Be consistent and constant in efforts to describe the "why" driving the decision for change. Have essential conversations and engage people on a personal level.
4. **Courageous to Champion Change** - Putting a plan or decision into effect requires silencing fear, worry and anxiety. Implementation is the courage to do the next thing well. **Timely change builds morale and diffuses critics.**
5. **Consistently Celebrate Wins** - Celebrate wins throughout the process of change. **See change through its completion to build and maintain credibility.**

Check your level of conviction and commitment before undertaking a transition. As a change agent, recognize change can be time-consuming, and there will be some people who will not be happy and may leave. Therefore, be secure in your convictions.

Conquer Cautiousness with Credible Choices

Cautious - Most of us purchase a new cell phone occasionally. I will abstain from Apple or Android conversations to say this. Whether you switch brands completely or upgrade a device, there are a plethora of changes. Chances are you research the best cell phone and plan for you and yours. Depending on age and technological capabilities, you might proceed to learn a new device with an air of caution. However, you make credible choices about what to learn. Then you pick up on how the smartphone can assist you in talking, texting, shopping, and so much more.

Credible - New ways of thinking in ministry are a must. Church and universities are experiencing continuous growth in online attendance. How will we reach children whose parents either do church online or are themselves unchurched? Kids and adults alike are looking for a reason to truly engage somewhere in the church, at school, or work. Are we giving people a reason to get connected when much of their engagement happens around sports, dance, or other groups of common interest within families?

Choices - If you are a more seasoned leader, are you willing to move over, share, and empower younger leaders? If you were once a Timothy, how well are you doing at being a Paul? Evaluate each age and stage of life. Rather than stifling new leaders, find ways to empower them. Young leaders need wisdom from seasoned leaders. Older leaders need innovative ideas of younger leaders. Win-wins are possible with credible choices. Seek first to understand before being understood.[5] Live a legacy; lead well now.

It takes diligence to overcome fear. **Complacency destroys from within**. Know there are letdowns; however, the more significant disappointment rests in knowing something should be done and not doing it. Trust your team to help overcome cautiousness. Embrace development, expansion, and progress.

Confident and Capable

Confident - The word confident and its close derivatives is used 54 times in the King James Version and 60 times in the New International Version.[6] It's all about our who, not people or our do. "Who we are in Christ" far supersedes what we do and the actions we take. Embrace and enjoy what's said about you in Philippians 1:6, *...being confident of this very thing, that he* *who began a good work in you will perform it until the day of Jesus Christ.*[7] Thankfully, our confidence isn't about our abilities or determination! We become increasingly powerful as we are led by the Spirit of God.

Real confidence comes from a relationship with Jesus Christ. When we place our trust in God, we will never be ashamed.[8] Hebrews 4:16 says we can approach the throne of grace with confidence during our time of help and need. You and God are a strong team together.[9] Fear reflects a lack of confidence in God and our self. Confidence is being positive about who you are and the very things you do while trusting God.

Capable - We help lead ministries and churches in places where many people no longer want to go or attend in a post-Christian America. Therefore, be open to learning new methods and strategies for reaching people in authentic and relevant ways. Your professional development as a leader rests with you. Watch YouTube, listen to podcasts, read, and find out what is happening in the world of Christian leadership and reaching people. Carey Nieuwhof, Craig Groeschel, and Reggie Joiner are just a few of the incredible catalysts helping navigate how to be the church in a digitally mobile and increasingly isolated age. Like we work on sharpening our mind, fitness, or skill set with our favorite hobby, we are to be even more adamant about learning how to reach the lost effectively. Being capable is about continually developing the qualities needed to love, reach, save, and disciple people differently than we ever have before.

Courageous Commitment

Courage can also be called "good cheer."[10] "The Greek word translated 'courage' and 'good cheer' means literally 'boldness and confidence.'"[11] Every time God instructs someone in the Bible to be strong, it's because a corresponding action awaits. **Being courageous *is* a call to action.**

Courageous - We see where Hezekiah trusted and relied on God. There was no other king in Judah like him before or after.[12] Queen Esther chose to speak up and save the Jewish people knowing it could cost her own life.[13] Both man and woman committed to pleasing God. Be courageous and lead out. **Action follows belief and trust in God.**

Two of my younger Texas friends are on a journey of courage. Hillary Evans and Becca Haskell worked at an orphanage in the Philippines. Their hearts broke as they saw sex trafficking take place where children were exchanged on a boat. Shortly afterwards a local Momma asked the American gals to raise her child. She no longer wanted to sell her daughter to others. The ladies became angry about the injustices of Filipino children. They learned of the UNICEF findings in 2016, noting 8 of 10 children in the Philippines are in danger of being sexually exploited online.[14] **Things that cause anger and pain are the very things we are called to change.**

> Things that cause anger and pain are the very things we are called to change.

One day back in the states, the girls grabbed a pizza and *viction*. They went through a journey packet where vision and action collided. Isaiah 61:1-4 became their foundation and child advocacy, their focal point. Within a year, they gave birth to Redeeming Zoe, where these women raised funds and headed to Cebu.

Redeeming Zoe provides skills to vulnerable children and families on how to protect themselves from exploitation. Afterschool programs show kids ways to build a safety net of protection. Prevention is happening as children make courageous reports to local officials. For more on Redeeming Zoe, go to https://www.redeemingzoe.org.

Courageous commitment looks different for everyone. The point is to put wings to the dreams in your heart. You're not waiting on others. God is waiting on you to cast vision and move forward in this ever-evolving journey.

Will You Commit? - The wake-up call for courageous commitment sounds the alarm. Yet leadership, at every level, hit the snooze button in 2011. David Kinnaman, president of Barna Research, shocked people in his book *You Lost Me* as we learned 59% of young adults from a Christian background left the church during their twenties. In 2019 Kinnaman published another book entitled *Faith for Exiles: 5 Ways for a New Generation to Follow Jesus in Digital Babylon*, indicating the church drop-out problem for young adults is an ever-increasing concern. "Nearly two-thirds of U.S. 18-29-year-olds who grew up in church tell Barna they have withdrawn from church involvement as an adult after having been active as a child or teen."[15]

Every Christ-follower in church, business, and education alike should fall to their knees at this moment, repent, and beg for mercy. We can't keep failing NextGen Kids. They need to experience Jesus personally.

Commitment - There must be a developmental mindset to where we are willing to explore ways and implement changes that engage non-traditional believers. Change can only take place when the church touches each member in a transformational way.

1. **Get Connected - Go beyond the four walls of a church building or organizational walls.** Outreach is not about placing door hangers and leaving a note asking people to attend a church service. It is about walking through any door to connect with people in a personal and meaningful way.
2. **Get Plugged In - Social Media is here to stay, and it's a way you can engage.** YouTube is the biggest social media platform, utilize it well. According to Pew Research, "Around three-quarters of U.S. adults (73%)

say they use YouTube, according to an early 2019 survey. And among 18-to24-year-olds, 90% say they use it. The only other social media platform that approaches YouTube in terms of its reach among Americans is Facebook, which was used by 69% of all adults as of early 2019."[16]
3. **Get Conversational** - Go beyond Sunday services and engage in conversations. Ask relevant questions in coffee shops and other gathering places in your area. Then do the same on social media. Add material to engage entire communities in your sphere of influence.

To lead change, we need to know how adaptable we are at embracing change personally. There are multiple free change assessments online. I would like to direct your attention to a free PDF change assessment from associate professor T. J. Denney at Purdue. The evaluation is a helpful leadership tool.

The link is https://www.ecfvp.org/uploads/tools/files/2_-change_readiness_assessment_0426111.pdf. The assessment will take less than 5 minutes to answer 35 questions. How you proceed afterward may take longer. ***Viction* embraces change.**

Cooperative, Considerate, and Conscientious

I find it ironic how some businesses cultivate servant leadership more than churches established 30 years or longer. Consider how Gaylord Hotels are cooperative, and Chick-Fil-A is considerate. Then there is Hobby Lobby and In and Out Burgers who are conscientious.

Cooperative - Maxie, my late husband, and I had reason to stay at several Gaylord hotels over the course of our marriage. Their guest services are impeccable. Call housekeeping for a box of tissue or anything else, and the response is "Consider it done." In answering, staff says this continuously throughout any stay. It's easy to believe because they remind you to, "Consider it done" often. If a hotel chain can build faith in customer service, how much more should we, as lovers of God, care for and be faithful to those around us so they can see Jesus?

Considerate - You know what they say at Chick-Fil-A, "It's my pleasure." You can slowly decide, change your order several times, or be having a bad day, yet they are going to flash you a genuine smile. When they are at work, they are "on point." Their culture shows it, and their attitude and voice say *it's genuinely their pleasure to serve you.*

Conscientious - Hobby Lobby unashamedly advertises products for Christmas and Easter Holidays with a Biblical emphasis. Much of their décor promotes a Christian perspective for daily living. In and Out Burgers openly celebrates Christ and the salvation message as John 3:16 is on the bottom of its cups and burger wrappers. It doesn't take people long to figure out their perspective on life.

Viction is where we pursue new vision and strategic action. ***Viction* reaches up to God and out to others with fresh intentionality and vitality.** Lose the Christianese verbiage. Express faith in words where pre-believers want to engage. Learn to resourcefully share biblical teachings while being immensely practical.

Can and Combat Cynicism - Celebrate Change

Can the Cynical - Most people pursue a call on their lives with great hope. They are upbeat and idealistic. Optimistic people are full of incredible ideas and can hardly sleep at night, considering all the ways they can help change lives. Then they experience disappointment. The letdowns happen here a little and there a little.

Cynicism does not walk up and tackle you. It slips in ever so gradually when you do not stop to grieve the loss in ministry. I'm not speaking about the death of an individual, although losing someone has a significant impact on any department.

The pain of loss happens when you pour into children, teens, or a family extensively, then they choose to leave. Perhaps they were not promoted to a position they desired fast enough. Maybe they felt as though they were not given enough attention in the local body. They could pick up an offense you didn't see coming. These and other situations can lead to the loss of friends and church members.

Disappointment is a part of loving others unconditionally. It becomes a stumbling block when we don't take time to grieve the hurt and ask God to heal open wounds. When we stifle raw emotions, they catch up and overtake us in time. Delayed grief morphs into either a calloused or cynical heart. The very core of such a leader stops seeing the best in people and tells why others won't change. Leaders seemingly can't recognize the hurt within themselves. A cynical individual pulls away from others to avoid more pain. Yet there are ways to soften brokenhearted leaders.

Combat Cynicism - First, recognize this is an issue. Ask God for help and receive freedom in this area. Then take the lead from kids and have a curious sense of wonder and fascination about life. Carey Nieuwhof reminds us, "Busyness is the enemy of wonder."[17] Next, allow yourself time to dream big and be creative. Permit yourself to do something playful each day. Engagement increases anticipation. Expectation helps take steps forward.

Celebrate Change - Part of the celebration is the actual preparation. The fundamental five of how to implement and celebrate change is helpful. Our very approach toward change signifies the chances for success.

1. **Pray and Fast** - This weakens the flesh and invites God to move mightily. Anything worth changing needs the right perspective.
2. **Write the Vision Down** - See and hear what God is saying. Keep it before you.
3. **Anticipate Where Opposition Can Occur** - Get on the defense to keep the enemy from scoring. Spiritual attacks seek to steal joy from the very purpose set before you. Be aware.
4. **Be Prepared and Stay Flexible** - Plan well, then make adjustments when needed. Read the climate to see how to best pace transitions.
5. **Celebrate Wins with People Often** - Since most people are initially resistant to change, honor past achievements while highlighting the advantages of change. Write down the wins as they occur. Applaud the process toward the end goal.

Be willing to go somewhere you have never been or do something you have never done; get ready to celebrate change. Then be ready to plan for transition, as it's progressive.

Viction: Where Vision and Action Collide

Strategic Solutions

- Choose to be cheerful in the midst of change.
- Change is profound, where a calm, cheerful countenance abounds.
- Conquer the past by focusing on the future.
- Realize the ones who lead change require great depth of character.
- Timely change builds morale and diffuses critics.
- See change through its completion to build and maintain credibility.
- Being courageous *is* a call to action.
- Action follows belief and trust in God.
- Things that cause anger and pain are the very things you are called to change.
- Know this; complacency destroys from within.
- *Viction* reaches up to God and out to others with new intentionality and vitality.
- *Viction* embraces change.
- Part of the celebration is in the actual preparation.
- Be willing to go somewhere you have never been and do something you have never done; get ready to celebrate change.

Cheering You On & Championing His Call!

Divine Insight
Choosing Christ & Cultivating Friendship:
_____
_____

Victionary Insight
Communicating Vision & Combining Action:
_____
_____

Team Insight
Connecting People & Creating Potential:
_____
_____

Young Leader Insight
Commending Talents & Celebrating Abilities:
_____
_____

Generational KidMin Insight
Cultivating Relationships & Collaborating Mentorships:
_____
_____

TIMELY TRANSITIONS

CHAPTER 5

T - Timely Transitions: Terrific, Tragic, Time-Outs, and Transformers

I will take my stand at my watchpost and station myself on the tower, and look out to see what he will say to me, and what I will answer concerning my complaint. And the Lord answered me: "Write the vision; make it plain on tablets, so he may run who reads it. For still the vision awaits its appointed time; it hastens to the end - it will not lie. If it seems slow, wait for it; it will surely come; it will not delay."[1]

"The Lord has always arranged my life so that I have to stay dependent on him. I just have to stay dependent because I have severe limitations."[2]

Teachable and Temperate

How to navigate through a transition as an individual, in church ministry and the workplace is possibly one of the most undertaught and overlooked processes in ministry care. Be teachable; it happens because even the best of leaders interchange the words change and transition. Yet each word involves two very different facets of leadership development and growth.

Transition Defined - Transition is what we are experiencing versus the change that happens to us, as discussed in the previous chapter. Transition is how we process and walk through the adjustment phase of change. **Timely transitions are how we reorient and go from how things used to be to how they are currently.**

Descriptions of the transition process developed by William Bridges Associates is most excellent. "Transition is the inner psychological process that people go through as they internalize and come to terms with the new situation that the change brings about. The starting point for dealing with transition is not the outcome but the endings that people have in leaving the old situation behind. Getting people through transition is essential if the change is actually to work as planned."[3]

> Change and transition are not interchangeable words.

There's probably an area of life where you are experiencing some form of transition even now. It's letting go of how things once were with either time, talents, or treasures. Transitions involve both learning and discovery; it's no accident that two American television channels use each of these words as their title. The names themselves are foretelling. There's The Learning Channel (TLC) and the Discovery Channel. Interestingly enough, they are both owned by the same company.

Truthful and Trustworthy

The William Bridges Transitional Model will be the foundation for much of this discussion regarding personal and transitional ministry transformations. This involves much more than change or changing positions. The three stages are Endings, The Neutral Zone, and New Beginnings.[4] For purposes of our leadership development personally and professionally, we will look at the transitional model through The Terrific, The

Tragic, Time-Outs, and The Transformers. The whole Children's Pastor vibe is coming through loud in this section for sure. The names and terminology are changed to "protect the innocent." The goal is to make a severe and, at times, sensitive discussion a little more palatable.

Terrific and Tragic

Terrific Transitions - The chapter title is telling. During my lifetime, I noted three stages of transition. Fantastic transitions are when an end to a season has come. It's the culmination of completing a particular phase or stage in life. **Terrific transitions are the end of something good that is climactic.** These events are mile markers and help set the course of life. Gradual progressions kids often celebrate are when they start school, turn double digits at ten, then thirteen as a teenager. For most, sweet sixteen is the time in the states to get a driver's license. High school graduations, associate degrees, technical schools, or college degrees are the culmination of something NextGen kids prepare and train for, then find it coming to a close in time.

This same completion rate of terrific transitions continues in more complex ways as some adults go on to earn advanced degrees at the master's or doctorate level, seminary, law school, or medical school. Culminating transitions happen as an expectant mother and couple go through pregnancy and have a child. In raising children there are multiple phases of transition to complete; then enters more new seasons.

Tragic Transitions - The closing of many transitions is celebratory, while others hold exceptionally bittersweet moments. Certain seasons come to an end prematurely with the loss of a parent, spouse, or child. Another loss happens when we lose something tied to other kinds of significance, including work, church, association, or affiliations that change in unexpected ways. These times cause us to examine ourselves and answer the question "Who am I?" **Guard your heart. Identity can quickly become attached to a person or what we do instead of who we belong to and what we are in Christ.**

The same is true spiritually. There are culminating moments that are no more. God opens and closes doors. Then there are times when the enemy comes in and steals something that belongs to us. In other instances, the close of a season happens due to our actions, whether positive or negative. With endings, we celebrate and grieve. **How we think and react to finalities is essential in how we enter a new season.**

Thoughtful Time-outs

Time-outs - There is another facet of transition we often deem as awful because we do not grasp what is going on. These are the seasons when you and I detect we are in a necessary time-out. It's the moments where we sense we have been put on a shelf and don't understand. We simply feel unproductive.

During this season, there is a significant disconnect from the past and often the present. Emotional numbness and detachment are descriptive of this particular transition. It can bring with it a sense of isolation to where being with people is not at the top of the priority list until we understand how to engage in the process. **Time-out moments and seasons serve as a reset button.** I have lived in this time-out zone more than one time in my life where it felt as though God would never use me again. It was terrifying until I understood this one thing. **Respite care is necessary to redirect**

> How we think and react to finalities is essential in how we enter a new season.

energy and resources. At this juncture embrace Psalm 18:2, *The Lord is my rock, my fortress and my deliverer; my God is my rock, in whom I take refuge, my shield and the horn of my salvation, my stronghold.*

Adult Time-outs - Before Maxie's death, the most recent time-out happened for me eight years ago. We were actively involved in one local church where we taught and served in multiple ways. I was over the women's ministry in a layperson's position, writing devotions, airing radio devotions weekdays, and having the time of my life.

Maxie and I knew that I was to go to Thailand with another church in town on a short-term mission trip that year to work with Life Impact International. I taught a women's Bible study at The Way Bible Church, using a book I wrote on Nehemiah. Over the next nine months, it became apparent that we were to leave our church home where we were married and move our membership to a church people referred to as "the one out in the middle of a pasture."

We were excited about the transfer until there were no more teaching or writing opportunities. For over a year, it seemed as though no one wanted us to volunteer. **God deliberately puts us in a sit and soak places periodically.** With a Type A personality, this felt less than fulfilling. Yet it would be vital for the things that would ensue over time.

Thriving Tenacity

Transformers - This season represents all things new and emerging. **Transpiring transitions mark the entryway into the future where new experiences await.** Embrace Isaiah 43:19, See, *I am doing a new thing! Now it springs up; do you not perceive it? I am making a way in the wilderness and streams in the wasteland.*

Further themes in life evolve during this season, along with unprecedented directional changes. This period represents all things fresh, novel, and different.

The time-out I experienced as we relocated to a new church brought forth several new seasons. It became clear I was to go back to school for ministry coursework. Volunteer and teaching opportunities gradually opened over the next two years. Then God called me out of 27 years in public education to become the full-time Children's Pastor at The Way Bible Church. Even though I knew I was in the midst of transition, I didn't see this one coming! It took significant confirmations for this bold new move.

Tests within Testimonies

Tales of Transition in Ministry - Transition is often a reference point of how to make the exchange from one lead pastor to another or how to navigate the void of one worship leader leaving while bringing in someone new. Therefore, churches and ministry organizations tend to look at change and transition as interchangeable words. However, the actions and effects of both of these facets of life are vastly different. Making change and ignoring transition is planning for success yet experiencing failure.

I have such an appreciation for the way the Episcopal Church Foundation (ECF) compares and contrasts transition and change. They provide an easy way to wrap our hearts and minds around the significant difference between transition and change.

Transition is the inward and spiritual responses, while change is the outward and visible event.[5] **Change is an event; transition is a process.**[6]

Teaching Time - The ECF uses two short, excellent illustrations that bear rephrasing and elaborating. Change is like moving to a new place. There are multiple intermediate steps. In some cases, an existing house needs to sell. Then choose items to pack and what to discard. There are additional choices to make as to whether friends will help you move or hiring a moving company. Utility transfers happen; kids may need to change schools, and then there is the inevitable last cleaning before leaving your existing residence. The last day arrives for you to be in your old home. Within the next day or two, depending on the length of the move, you will be residing in a different home that is new to you. All these changes are about getting from one locale to another.

Team Time - The same application is valid for churches, ministries, and organizations who are growing, mobile, changing locations, or are undergoing expansion programs. A psychical move represents change; it's overtly visible. **Change is about moving from one location, place, or situation to another.**

Transition is more about the journey within the new home or space where change has taken place. We have moved into three different houses in the last sixteen years. The actual moves took place within a day. Making the house a home took much longer. Why? Inevitably, certain items no longer work in the new spaces, or different furnishings become more functional. There are times when the design of a house calls for something special in the nesting process. **The journey is progressive.**

Team Time - The journey of each individual is much the same way. The mind, will, and emotions need time to respond and develop new and different patterns of how emotional, psychological, and spiritual needs get met in spirit, soul, and body. No one can move into the new without leaving the old behind. Think about this; there's the distance between the old and new houses. Some distances are short and well-traveled. Other journeys are longer and have winding roads with steep inclines. **The type of ending a person or organization experiences factors into their uniquely personal**

transitional and transformative experience. When coupled with people traveling at a different speed, give grace in the place. It could end up being your journey one day.

Above all, refuse to be shallow and act like the journey isn't a reality. Be personable and ask questions within your team and to members in the church. Visit about what's ended. Find out what's helpful in the transition. Discuss predictors of how people can know when things are becoming healthy again.

Thoughtful and Tentative

Maxie has been deceased nine months as of writing this chapter. His death leaves a massive void. I'm a verbal processor. The very person who listens well and shares ideas is no longer in my home. I've had to learn new ways to receive validation as it no longer comes from him. To show you how much redirecting and retraining is taking place, I'll share two more quick examples.

I never look or listen to weather reports; Maxie was an incessant weather watcher. He gave multiple updates in person, through calls, or texts. I knew how to dress for the day as he gave me a run-down first thing every morning. The updates kept me safe in travel and helped me understand when plans should be adjusted. I'm deliberately making myself use a weather app, but oh how I miss cute personalized weather reports.

More importantly, I no longer have a life partner who's excited about the things of God, covering me in prayer and standing in spiritual battles with me. I miss his protective prayers and the cover of a blessing he spoke over my life. I remind myself; God is my truly great husband. Yet I miss the deep voice who prayed me through.

The transition for people involved at any level as a church member, volunteer, or staff experiences the same types of psychological and spiritual journeys where change is required.

Transition is an entirely different ballgame when fresh ways are needed to fill big voids that are new and incredibly awkward. Be considerate and thoughtful in assisting others as they embrace the new journey. **Help people discover where God's moving even when there's pain.**

Titles to Track

There are credible resources, withstanding the test of time, addressing transition with individuals or organizations. One such book is written by William and Susan Bridges entitled *Managing Transitions: Making the most of Change Transitions*. There are exceptional articles on the William Bridges Associates website at https://wmbridges.com. Go to the Resources tab, then click on "Articles." In "Getting Them Through the Wilderness" William Bridges describes how effective leaders can navigate change and transition with excellence using the journey seen in the story of Moses. The leadership classic *Transitions: Making Sense of Life's Changes* is an easy read yet incredibly profound. This resource is available in multiple formats.

Triumphant in Transitions

The 2019 movie *Overcomer* is a Christian drama about an asthmatic girl named Hannah Scott, whose love of running is one thing she likes to do.[7] Hannah is being raised by her grandmother, who tells her both parents are deceased, yet Hannah has unanswered questions about her Dad. The movie has twists and turns where Hannah finds herself on a journey.

Through an incidental yet divine connection, her inexperienced coach John Harrison befriends a diabetic blind man in the hospital. As their friendship grows, new information unfolds about Hannah's Dad. If you haven't watched the movie, here's your *spoiler alert warning*.

This young girl experiences a painful transition with the loss of her parents. A traditional family is no longer an option. She has a terrific development in the fact that her maternal grandmother can provide for and raise Hannah from a very young age.

The time-out comes in Hannah's life when she seems to have no real meaning or joy. Nothing is making sense to her, and she has questions with no answers. Then transformational moments occur, bringing both conflict and joy. In this heart-gripping tale, Hannah discovers her terminally ill Father is alive. She has limited opportunities to meet with him, where the love of cross-country running is a shared reality.

As Hannah works through the transitions going on in her life, she chooses to forgive her Father. Throughout the course of the racing season, transformation happens in relationships and experiences.

Anticipation in the transition process helps navigate each journey with greater intentionality. **Become conscious of the seasons in life.** In *Didn't See It Coming,* Carey Nieuwhof shares how to overcome the seven most significant challenges that no one expects and everyone experiences. Wisdom is at our fingertips. Slow down, read, digest, and apply. The best thing you can do for yourself and others is to study the seasons of life and their predictability. Recognize the signs and heed the instruction. There's a transformer in you raring to go and equip people.

Viction: Where Vision and Action Collide

Strategic Solutions

- Transitions are the most undertaught and overlooked processes in ministry care.
- Timely transitions are how we reorient and go from how things used to be to how they are currently.
- Recognize there's probably an area of life where you are experiencing some form of transition even now.
- Terrific transitions are the end of something good that is climactic.
- Guard you heart. Identity can quickly become attached to a person or what we do instead of who we belong to and what we are in Christ.
- How we think and react to finalities are essential in how we enter a new season.
- Time-out moments and seasons serve as a reset button.
- Respite care is necessary to redirect energy and resources.
- God deliberately puts us in sit and soak places periodically.
- Transpiring transitions mark the entryway into the future where new experiences await.
- Change and transition are not interchangeable words.
- Transition is the inward and spiritual responses, while change is the outward and visible event.[8]
- Change is an event; transition is a process.[9]
- Change is about moving from one location, place, or situation to another.
- Transition is more about the journey within the new home or space where change has taken place.
- The journey is progressive.
- Help people discover where God's moving even when there's pain.
- Become conscious of the seasons in life.

Cheering You On & Championing His Call!

Divine Insight
 Choosing Christ & Cultivating Friendship:
 _____
 _____

Victionary Insight
 Communicating Vision & Combining Action:
 _____
 _____

Team Insight
 Connecting People & Creating Potential:
 _____
 _____

Young Leader Insight
 Commending Talents & Celebrating Abilities:
 _____
 _____

Generational KidMin Insight
 Cultivating Relationships & Collaborating Mentorships:
 _____
 _____

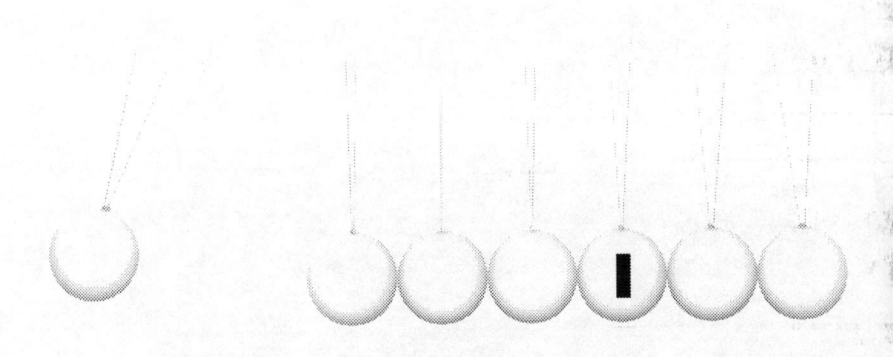

IMPECCABLE INDIVIDUALIZATION

CHAPTER 6

I - Impeccable Individualization: Equip the People

In everything set them an example by doing what is good. In your teaching show integrity, seriousness and soundness of speech that cannot be condemned, so that those who oppose you may be ashamed because they have nothing bad to say about us.[1]

"Jesus loves us so much that He will never keep us small. In Him, absolutely nothing is impossible: There are no limits".[2]

Importance of Influence

Importance - In looking at the importance of influence, let's look at each word then view their power together. First, let's start by honoring the essential individuals who pour into your life. You know, the people, regardless of what age or stage, believe in you and make you feel exceptional. There's a relative who you connect with exceptionally well. There are those at school, church, or community events whose words and actions change how you see yourself and the world in a positive light.

Igniters - There are Sunday School teachers whose friendliness and kindness endeared me to their hearts. Mr. and Mrs. Williams took the time to find out what I liked personally. Their goodness readily extended to my Momma. When I walked into Mrs. Nada Crouch's room, she acted like I was the sun and the moon. Her smiles and hugs affirmed my value and worth in elementary school. As a preteen, helping in Bus Ministry at church meant the world to me. Jim Haney filled in the gaps as a father figure. Throughout school, teachers wrote on the pages of my life. Several of them wrote chapters. Mr. Newsom, Mr. Taylor, and Mrs. Roberts helped shape my integrity, work ethic, love of books, and writing throughout public school.

Inspiring Individuals - Stop and think of a person or people who hold a place of significance in your life. List them in the margin if you like to write in books. Commonalities will emerge. Influential people are those who invest time in our lives. They are interested in who you are, what you care about, and how you go about achieving results. **Extraordinary people are those who care about your story.**

Individualize - Conversely, what makes you essential in the lives of others is your interest in them as a person. Go beyond surface questions, and get to personal likes, interests, and dreams. A child may be saving to buy the latest most excellent game. For young adults, it could be about getting a job, finding a spouse, or starting a family. More seasoned people may want to share about transitions, kids getting married, grandkids, or hobbies. Our social media-driven society has made it easier than ever to duck out of genuine conversations. Do yourself and others a favor, don't. **Individualize your discussions. It's what people really want and rarely receive.**

Care; genuinely care about what's spoken.
Understand; learn from the person.
Smile and engage in the conversation.
Talk WAY LESS and listen more.
Open-ended questions drive genuine conversations.
Motivate them with encouraging words as they share.
In focus by being engaged with approachable body language.
Zealous about life and the potential you see in them.
Eye contact is one form of respect that's appreciated.
Leave the conversation to where the other person is glad

they got to visit with you. Help recharge their battery; they will want to do the same thing for others as will you.

Influence - You and your teams have a sphere of influence; it's the ability to motivate and inspire those around you. Interestingly enough, some of these traits listed in customizing conversations cross over into being a person of influence. Having stable character traits discussed in chapter 2 of *Viction* is paramount as a baseline. Past that, the questions are, what and how are you using your sphere of influence?

Intentionality - In their book *Becoming a Person of Influence*, John Maxwell and Jim Dornan discuss what it takes if you want to lead well. You need to be intentional about gaining influence.[3] Authentic leadership is where people seek your advice. They trust you; therefore, they can follow your lead. Their book discusses nine core qualities essential to making a difference in the lives of others. A person of influence walks in integrity, nurtures, believes in, and listens to people. They understand people and desire to help them succeed in a variety of ways of including connecting and empowering them to be their very best. When we help others achieve, they reproduce influencers. Legacy of this nature changes the culture of families, communities, states, nations, and continents.

Importance of Influence - You guessed it. The importance of influence is getting yourself off of your sweet mind and focusing on helping others. Information is more accessible now than ever. Content is available through podcasts, websites, YouTube, and a barrage of other social media platforms. **People are not craving more content; they are already overwhelmed by the sheer amount of information coming at them every day. People are starving for someone to come alongside them to help show them the way to lift the load and help them get to where they are going.**

Decide who needs to get your time and why. Be intentional when investing in others. You can't help everyone, everywhere, all at once. **Be intentionally specific about who you will assist and why.** Stay in your wheelhouse; then, you will be able to motivate and empower others. You genuinely help people in areas where you are most passionate.

Interactive Instruction

No one likes being talked at or lectured to when learning. People hunger to learn and are accepting when preaching, teaching, and training is clear, concise, and engaging. Go beyond describing how to do something. Roll up your sleeves and show another person through an experience together. Working together on even a small project can make all the difference.

Hands-on learning creates intentional memories while creating a culture of trust. The experience can be working on a car, building a kite, baking a main dish, or making bows for presents. On a side note, I *will* join in for a how to make bows lesson. Instruction in ministry and education organizations often focuses on teaching a concept, method, principle, or strategy in how to achieve the desired outcome. Keep it simple. **Use concrete examples to help explain what many may perceive to be abstract concepts.** Instruction in any field, especially ministry, is all about helping others. I like how my pastor, Doctor Joel Tiemeyer says it, "Take systematic theology throughout the Bible and make it practical Christianity that applies to situations in everyday life."

Giving instruction is meant to be enjoyable, fun and engaging for the learner and teacher. Visuals and demonstrations help share information with others effectively. **Teach and reteach by doing something together, then help others prepare to share.** Notice the most effective sermons, teachings, and sessions with groups is when they're engaging and interactive

to where people are doing something to reinforce their learning. "The Cone of Learning" by Edgar Dale suggests we remember:[4]
- 5% of what we hear
- 10% of what we read
- 20% of what we hear and read
- 30% of what we are shown
- 50% of what we discuss
- 75% of what we do
- 90% of what we teach others

Individualize Instruction

Just remember, it was my first year of teaching in a tiny 1A school system in rural east Texas. This account could sound a little archaic. At the time, the elementary school was an open classroom concept. There were dividers between each classroom, yet they did not go all the way to the ceiling. My first assignment was to teach special education. There again, it was a small school, so at any given time, there could be students in the room from first grade to twelfth grade working on at least three or more subjects. Let me say Gwenn Patrick is a saint of a Teacher's Assistant who will have many crowns in heaven. The instruction was specific to each child, so a lot was going on. The point is this. You can teach in such a way where everyone learns at their level of need, speed, and growth simultaneously.

Multisensory Learning - There are effective teaching strategies available to help equip kids and adults for genuine life change based on their individual needs. There is the multisensory approach using two or more of the senses. Some people learn best with their eyes as a visual learner. Others learn well by listening. Another mode of learning is through touch or tactile learning. For others, body movements, referred to as kinesthetic learning, helps process information better.

Scaffold Instruction - In the education world, this

word describes how to build learning based on an individual's current understanding. Meet a child, teen, or adult where they are through experiences and knowledge they currently have. They model and practice what they know, then a new strategy is introduced where the learner can apply what they have learned previously. For we know, it's precept upon precept, line upon line, here a little and there a little that comes into play.[5]

Tailored Instruction - Find out the unique interests of people and tailor or customize activities that incorporate their interest. Jesus used practical examples when teaching. He met people right where they were. If a group of kids is into sports, activities could include sports' illustrations. If you live in a community where farming is the main focus, the example will involve livestock and other things of **interest to people who live in a specific area or region.**

Pace Instruction - This requires great flexibility. Some people move fast, while others are more steady. Quick learners may need extra motivators in messages or activities. Steady people may need more time. **Meet people where they are and help them get to where they want to go.**

I believe anyone can learn something when sharing information in a way that's of interest to them. The keyword here is interest when thinking about student ministry. With adults, the concept leans more to buy-in. Business and education circles refer to this as "the hook." It's what causes people to engage.[6] **Always be on the lookout for "the hook" where people will want to know more.** Young leaders are highly innovative. Trust them for fresh ideas on how to teach, train, and lead.

Inspiring Inscriptions and Initiatives

Impart - Letter writing is almost a lost art. However, people enjoy and remember when they receive written words of encouragement. It's far better than receiving bills in the mail. Some of the most influential leaders I know, start their day by writing notes. They send cards expressing appreciation for something that took place in the last twenty-four hours.

Intent - Writing a note does not have to be lengthy to be meaningful. Start with a greeting using the person's name. When the card is more informal and personal, I tend to start with a positive adjective or attribute describing the person with the same letter as their first name. I write this book to where each chapter focuses on a particular letter of the alphabet with keywords and supporting phrases spelling out *VICTION*. It reinforces learning and helps with memory recognition and word association.

Individual - I look for every opportunity to speak life. For instance, the note may start with Lovely Lynda or Anointed Allan. Express a specific thought you want to share in three to five sentences. End the correspondence with a complimentary close like best regards, respectfully yours, or something expressing your heart toward the person receiving the postcard, note, or card. In many instances, I close with you are loved by The King and me. Then I sign my name. Remind people of their worth and value.

> Little individualized touches
> make a BIG difference.

Invite - Ask God into the situation. What does *HE* want to say to them through you? His heart on the matter builds up, encourages, and uplifts like no other. You and I have the privilege of being instruments for His use, purpose, and glory. We get to be the hands and feet of Jesus, WOW!

Impact - Several years back, I received a card on my birthday. The envelope was more substantial in size than usual. The husband and wife duo spent time writing out at least twenty or more descriptive words beginning with the letter S for Sherry. They hand-delivered the card and waited to see my expression. Their comment was, "It means so much to us when you attach meaning to our names. We wanted to do the same for you." **Little individualized touches make a BIG difference.**

Invigorate - One friend, in particular, keeps thank you cards readily available on the corner of his desk. It's important to note that people who practice this art are some of the most appreciative and grateful individuals on the planet. They have lots of joy because they are continuously focusing on the good in others and the circumstances around them.

Initiate - Go beyond the text message in expressing appreciation and touching base with people. Write on a page in their heart. Most of us keep a cell phone nearby. Pick it up and make the call. Give a word of encouragement and let them know God cares, and you do too. These calls do not take long at all. You will typically want to limit the length of the conversation to be respectful of everyone's time. Yet the initiative on your part will be truly impactful and meaningful for the recipient. The dialogue encourages you to fight the good fight of faith too. A call is an excellent break in their otherwise very labor-intensive day. When they don't answer, leave a message. They can listen to it over and over again when encouragement is needed or wanted. **Be deliberate; then you become a powerhouse of strength and support for the people around you.**

Invest in Individuals

Investment Option #1 – Individualized experiences are what people are craving. You can invest money and time on multiple objects tailored to individuals. Everywhere you look, products and services are more personalized than ever.

Single servings in the marketplace are prevalent. People are paying big money to have services uniquely prepared just for them. Meal preps ship to homes along with household goods and specialized clothing. Consumers want personal attention anywhere they go.

Investment Option #2 - Ministry meets a person at their point of need. Large scale services, programs, and activities all have their rightful place and are beneficial for building up the body of Christ. Yet there is so much more to offer. **Spending resources *on people* carry the most significant rewards and dividends.** People seek authentic relationships. How will they ever know how big our God is if they can't see Him in the moments of everyday life where we interact with one another?

Initial Investment - Investing in people begins by hearing another person's story one-on-one or in small group settings. This helps in knowing how to pray and where to help. Even social media is making small group on-line conversations more accessible and advantageous for groups who share common interests.

Interest Compounded - Periodically, I reread Gary Chapman's book entitled *The Five Love Languages*[7] or review my notes from the book. I need the reminder that how I naturally communicate love to someone may not be the way they receive love. Over the years, I have come to realize that love languages can change over time as well. Chapman categorizes the five love languages as being:[8]

1. *Words of Affirmation* - Verbal or written words thrill this person.
2. *Acts of Service* - Actions speak louder than words for this individual.
3. *Receiving Gifts* - Thoughtful and meaningful gifts touches this person.

4. *Quality Time* - Undivided attention with no multitasking shows love.
5. *Physical Touch* - Appropriate touch based on relationship.

Understanding your love language and being insightful about how others receive love can make a big difference when investing in people. It helps you know that a gentle touch on the shoulder means nothing to someone who receives love and validation through words of affirmation. In observing people, how they give love is often the way they receive love too. Take the time and get to know someone; then, you can identify how to invest in a person more effectively.

Instrumental Intercession

Intercede - It's so easy for people to feel as though they have slipped through the cracks, and no one notices them. I've experienced those feelings before; it's a slippery slope. It's good to invest in individuals with time and resources. Yet the more important and significant works are done in prayer, specific prayer, to be exact.

Inquire - Begin by asking God how to pray for people. The more you seek to know His heart for people, the more He will reveal Himself. Standing in the gap for someone is powerful because heaven and earth begin moving on their behalf. God can do in moments what it takes man or woman years to accomplish.

If you don't hear a specific direction in how to pray for someone, stop and get grateful. Praise God for the things He is doing, both great and small. Then spend moments worshipping God. We enter His presence with bold confidence.[9] Yet, it is essential to remember that He created us for fellowship with Himself.[10]

Intimate - My sister Lynda is a prayer warrior, much like our Mother and Maternal Grandmother. She spends much time in His presence and hosting His presence. One of the sweetest things she shared recently was this. "The main thing is that He wants to hear our voice. He wants to see *our* face. If He wants to see our face, we have to be facing Him and guess what we see?"

Impact

Impact can be compared to making an impression in clay, little hands have to touch the clay multiple times to make an imprint. Remember, it often takes multiple moments with people and many small imprints to make an impact that lasts throughout eternity.

Just as well-rounded character produces great leaders, so does individualization that addresses the whole person's spirit, soul, and body. Impact answers the question, how will this advance the kingdom of God? If it doesn't, you're wasting your time and effort. Be intentional. Ask God, what do you want to do through me today?

Your personal impact and organizational impact drive the work and ministry, not the other way around. Refuse to shrink back because something may take extra work or effort.

Strategic Solutions

- Extraordinary people are those who care about your story.
- Customize conversations; it's what people really want and rarely receive.
- People are not craving more content; they are already overwhelmed by the sheer amount of information coming at them every day.
- People are starving for someone to come alongside them to help show them the way to lift the load and help them get to where they are going.
- Be intentionally specific about who you will help and why.
- Use concrete examples to help explain what many may perceive to be abstract concepts.
- Teach and reteach by doing something together, then help others prepare to share.
- Meet people where they are and help them get to where they want to go.
- Always be on the lookout for "the hook" where people will want to know more.
- Little individualized touches make a BIG difference.
- Be deliberate; then you become a powerhouse of strength and support for the people around you.
- Spending resources on people carry the most significant rewards and dividends.
- Your personal impact and organizational impact drive the work and ministry not the other way around.
- Refuse to shrink back because something may take extra work or effort.

Viction: Where Vision and Action Collide

Cheering You On & Championing His Call!

Divine Insight
Choosing Christ & Cultivating Friendship:

_____

_____

Victionary Insight
Communicating Vision & Combining Action

_____

_____

Team Insight
Connecting People & Creating Potential:

_____

_____

Young Leader Insight
Commending Talents & Celebrating Abilities:

_____

_____

Generational KidMin Insight
Cultivating Relationships & Collaborating Mentorships:

_____

_____

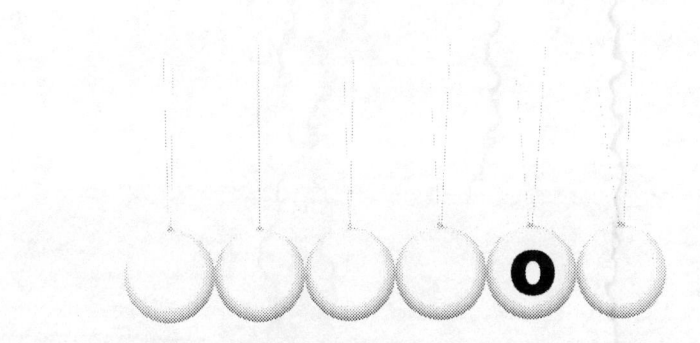

OPTIMIZING AND OVERCOMING OBSTACLES

CHAPTER 7

O - Optimizing and Overcoming Obstacles

Be strong and courageous. Do not fear or be in dread of them, for it is the Lord your God who goes with you. He will not leave you or forsake you.[1]

"If, per chance you are confronted by a discourager, do not let him derail your destiny. Very graciously let him know your eyes are fixed on God, who specializes in doing the impossible."[2]

Optimistic Overflow

Whether in the jungles of Africa, the oceanside villages in the Philippines, the mountains in Thailand, Mexico, and Costa Rica or among the pine trees in east Texas, I find one thing in common with those who know how to overcome life's obstacles and optimize their daily living. Optimistic people are not without troubles; they simply choose their attitude. They understand, *hope deferred makes the heart sick, but a desire fulfilled is a tree of life.*[3] There is a belief deep within that God is good; therefore, life is good. Positive people simply do the next thing with every ounce of joy in their being. **When there is a smile in your heart, it shows on your face.** Optimism is the perfect breeding ground for *viction*.

***Viction* is the euphoria of seeing a vision, with action steps for the process ahead.** A blank canvas is not overwhelming to an artist; it is full of the potential for a masterpiece in the making. Your life is a masterwork in production. There is a myriad of gorgeous colors on your canvas. If you stare at one section for too long, you will become limited to the color pallet of the moment. Take a step back and see great beauty. Get it settled inside yourself,

> I have much worth.
> > I have terrific promise.
> > > I have great potential.
> > > > I have tremendous value.
> > > > > I have great clarity as I hear and see God's direction.

Even though I am 5'13" or 6'1" in height for those who are mathematical savvy, my maternal grandmother was adorable and petite at 5'2". Grandma Lela battled pneumonia multiple times, survived breast cancer, and numerous other difficulties throughout her life. Yet, her outlook was very joyful. She whistled all the time, had a pep in her step when she walked and beheld beauty in everything around her, especially birds. She liked the sound of a Bob White bird in particular. Grandma Lela was confident of this, "God takes care of the birds, and he takes care of me."[4] **You have the unique ability to choose in your heart what you believe about yourself.**

Orderly and On-Point Organization

Overcoming Obstacles - A trouble-free life is unrealistic. To overcome an obstacle, we start by identifying the problem or feeling. Ask God to show you creative solutions. After getting His perspective, develop a plan. Track your progress of working through the situation. Being debt-free, living a healthy lifestyle, and recovering from devastating loss is all possible. It begins with baby steps. Just take the first step. Then take one more as you can when you can. Let's do this knowing that what the enemy meant to destroy us; God will turn into triumph.[5]

Optimizing Output - A dear friend said it to me for so long, I repeat it now myself, "Cleanliness is next to Godliness." To be honest, *VICTION* requires organization. Everything has a place, and everything in its place deals with more than just physical stuff. **Chaos is where the enemy wreaks havoc.** Therefore, we are to be proactive, physically, mentally, and spiritually.

Physically - When I have allowed my schedule to get too busy or one or more areas are out of order, I start bringing balance back into the situation by choosing three aspects of life I want to move forward within the hour. At the beginning of this hour, I deal with doing the least favorable task at hand. You know what I'm referencing, the item on the To-Do list that quickly gets pushed back due to dread or procrastination. By starting, you will have already won half the battle.

In the next twenty minutes I turn my focus to something more on the "I can do" side of things. It's not bothersome; it merely needs to get taken care of now. In the last third of this target hour, I turn my attention to something I look forward to doing. It serves as the reward for doing the more tedious tasks first. Working with bite-sized chunks of time diffuses the feeling of being overwhelmed. The visual in words looks like this:

20 minutes	**Choose to do**
20 minutes	**Can do**
20 minutes	**Look forward to**

Twenty minutes may not reorganize an entire kitchen. It's enough time to load the dishwasher and wipe down the counters, clean the refrigerator, or restock the coffee bar. **When entering a space, it helps to clean from left to right. Order avoids retracing steps, and progress is**

apparent in a short amount of time. The same principle is applicable at work and in ministry when it comes to completing tasks. Twenty minutes may not clean out an entire file cabinet but is can declutter one drawer.

Mentally - The same is true mentally. Much mental fatigue exists because we think we are focusing on the task at hand, yet many thoughts are floating through our mind about a dozen different things.

Deliberately choose to close what's running in the background of your mind. When something is playing continuously like background music or a movie picture, yet it's in your brain, that's worry trying to steal your joy. Shut it down.

Random thoughts use energy continuously, like open apps on a cell phone. When multiple apps are running at once, the battery drains much quicker. Close the apps in your mind. Mental clarity requires focus. When a thought comes to mind in another area that may need attention, make a note of it and return to the project at hand. The note section of my cell phone is in and of itself a file cabinet helping me know what needs attention and when.

Spiritually - Fill your heart with good things. Out of the abundance of the heart, the mouth speaks.[6] Every ounce of overflow comes from the heart. If you feel depleted at the moment in any area, it's a heart issue. It shows when we have not guarded our heart.[7]

How do we take care of our heart? We flood it with God's word; then, we don't sin against Him or ourself.[8] The heart is mentioned more than 800 times in the Old Testament. Motives matter. Because spirit, soul, and body are three in one, just like Father, Son, and Holy Spirit, each area is interconnected and needs to flourish for you to be at your optimum. Balance of these three is the key to an orderly life where we can enjoy a vibrant relationship with God and love others as He does.

Ongoing Order - A pitfall to organizing can be thinking, "alright, everything's orderly; don't touch anything!"

Organization in and of itself is not the end goal; it is the springboard for higher productivity and an enjoyable life where you do not have to keep redoing fundamental things over and over again. Find what works for you.

Observable Opportunities

Observant - The most significant obstacle, not seeing opportunities everywhere around you. God is so good to place people in our lives who can help carry out your God-given passion. Likewise, you hold giftings and talents someone genuinely needs to succeed and go to the next level.

Remember, the nudge of the Holy Spirit is frequently gentle. He may be leading you to visit with someone or do something, and it makes absolutely no sense to you. Tell your logic to behave and be quiet. Follow the promptings. You know, the still small voice that, if not careful, can be dismissed as a random thought. Fine-tune your hearing. **Opportunities are everywhere.** Beyond fine-tuning, be quick to obey. When we are not hearing God with high frequency, we need to go back to the last time we heard Him speak and give direction. Then determine if we are fully obedient.

Opportunities - Part of operating in *viction* is doing noble acts of kindness consistently. We have specific instructions about how to optimize opportunities. It begins at a very relational level.

1. Respect and love your parents well. *Honor your Father and Mother.*[9] God will reward you with a long healthy life if you do.
2. Do good by your friends and your parent's friends. I appreciate this rendering of the scripture. *Don't forget your friend or your parent's friend.*[10] Befriending

is powerful, especially about your parent's friends. **Our lack of *viction* may very well be blocking incredible opportunities God wants us to see and access.**
3. Do good to *everyone*, especially those in the household of faith.[11]
4. Speak evil of no one, avoid quarreling, be gentle, and show perfect courtesy toward all people.[12]
5. Live at peace with everyone, as far as it depends on you.[13]

Even while writing this section, I am under conviction about walking out Titus 3:2. We have opportunities to live and lead well in word and deed.

Open-Hearted - Dare to take a chance and ask some questions of yourself regarding ideas and interests you long to see come to life. **Be willing to ask the "what if" questions with anticipation rather than fear.** What if I succeed? What if this makes a difference in the lives of people? What if I was born to do this? Dare to dream without limitations! Why? **We have an infinite God who is not bound by our puny limitations.** Three more questions worth the asking. Why not me? Why not here? Why not now? **Life is not about limitations; it is about optimization. Change your vantage point.**

Offer - I know of a couple who has been looking at some land for a while. They found a spread that met all the criteria of their dreams, yet it was not for sale. The owner had not been willing to sell for quite some time. The husband approached the owner a year later. The response this time was, "I've always liked you. Think I want to sell it to you." The owner had turned down an offer from another individual just days before. Interesting how God's favor steps in and makes a way when the owner had refused to sell earlier. **Make the ask. God is just waiting to fling doors wide open for you, his favorite child.** I certainly am glad He has lots of favorites!

Viction: Where Vision and Action Collide

Outstanding is Obtainable

There's a few of our young granddaughters, AKA Grands, who tell almost any story with this beginning, "When I was a little girl..." in this instance, I follow their lead. When I was a little girl, we moved to Sulphur Springs, Texas one summer. A pilot program called Head Start was new. I attended every day. My teacher's name was Mrs. Cotton; she was a very stately looking African American lady who had a long wooden pointer stick. The teacher would ask me my name, and I would say, "Harry." I had a speech impediment. She worked with me daily to help me pronounce my name correctly, SSSSSHHHHH - E - R - R - Y. She was even more determined about two other goals.

Multiple times each day, Mrs. Cotton would use a long wooden pointer and go tap, tap, tap on the first glass encased framed diploma. Then she would say loudly, slowly and clearly, "You WILL get a high school diploma." I thought, OK. I just had a brother and sister graduate from high school; I will do that too. Then Mrs. Cotton would take two steps over and point to a much larger framed diploma as we sat in a classroom at Lamar Elementary School. Then there would be another series of clicks that were even louder than before, CLICK, CLICK, CLICK. She would look at each of us in the eyes while she spoke, "YOU - WILL - GO - TO - COLLEGE - AND - GET - A - DIPLOMA."

I liked Mrs. Cotton, yet I had an absolute reverent fear of her when she spoke about diplomas. She said to go; at age six, I was already going to college in my heart and mind. She made a believer out of me in less than six weeks that summer.

> Situations do not define you, your choices do.

Four university diplomas later, I seem to enjoy life-long

learning even though good grades were not critical to me in public school. Although a piece of paper does not define you or in itself give you worth or value, the words of Mrs. Cotton resonated loudly to where I knew outstanding is obtainable in any area of life.

I wasn't sure about the move to a new town, or my parents getting divorced in an era when it seemed taboo. I also did not understand why my dad walked away from the ministry, my mom, and me. I did understand Mrs. Cotton. Words are powerful. **Situations do not define you, your choices do.** What do you perceive as outstanding? Excellence begins by taking one step at a time. **Go after your goals and dreams with great resolve.** While you are at it, make sure to pour into others' lives too.

Onward Olympian!

Jennifer, one of our darling daughters, walked into the house one day in high school and asked us, "May I try out for the Cross-Country Team?" We agreed. The one stipulation, when she ran alone, I would follow behind her in our vehicle. Over the years, we went to many cross-country races. I have such an appreciation for runners, their discipline, and perseverance.

Three years ago, I walked and hardly jogged the Hot Chocolate Race in Dallas, Texas; this same daughter was on a long-distance run in another state. I finished what was a long 5K race for me as I did it toward the end of a forty-day water fast. The pace, terrible; the victory, triumphant. The obstacle, doing something that took physical exertion when my body was weak. On the way back to the parking lot, Jennifer calls; I hear her voice, uh-oh. Listen to Jennifer's story unfold as every obstacle is dealt with in the valley of decision.

"The coolness of the February morning was balanced by the warmth of the sun. With shoes laced snug and a smile on my face, I began my coveted long run through the countryside. Middle Tennessee is beautiful at any time of the year. Nature entrances me, and running enables me to see, feel, and taste it all at once.

Running had been a part of me in varying degrees since high school. This Saturday morning was no different. It was my time to move through space and time on foot, releasing my mind to fly. When I started my watch to track the miles, I immediately felt exhilarated. My thoughts drifted to the end of my first marathon just two months prior. Under-trained and uniformed, my finish time reflected the extreme pain I felt in my muscles. Ouch! After 15 minutes of lying on the ground following my agonizing 26.2-mile finish, I knew I would revisit the distance. My unfinished business with running was at the sprouting stage of growth. My heart knew that my legs had tremendous more potential. A spark ignited. Qualifying for the prestigious Boston Marathon instantly attached itself to my dreams. Then, reality bit hard!!

A mile into my morning run, three Australian Shepherd dogs dashed across the road toward me. Two usually friendly dogs showed an evil side with an aggressive third dog. Unable to grab my pepper spray in time, the most massive dog knocked me down and clamped down on my calf with a vengeance while the other two nipped my ankles in between angry barks. My fight instinct kicked in high gear. Somehow, I managed to free myself from their teeth and jump off the ground to limp away. The owners, who had been screaming at their dogs the whole time, were finally able to restrain their pets. But the damage had been done.

My throbbing calf doubled in size and oozed blood. I could barely walk. Hot tears begrudgingly rolled down my cheek. After an unwanted trip to an emergency clinic, I found myself lying on the couch at home. I felt numb. What now? Mentally, I found myself at crossroads. Was I a fighter or a quitter? Would I fight to trust? Would I fight to believe? Would I fight to stay the course? If God really works ALL things for His glory and our good, would I follow His roadmap to success? I knew the answer. I had seen tangible evidence of God's faithfulness and goodness from an early age. In those frail moments on the couch, unable to walk, I prayed for His strength to engulf my weakness.

After a month of believing without seeing and hoping without feeling, I was able to resume running. A new fire burned in my soul. Little did I know that I would need that fire to light the way through four months of darkness six months later. 'Overcome the quit through the power of the cross' became my mantra. As a hobbyist songwriter, I could not help but weave together a song to help me remember. The bridge continues to echo through my being: 'The cross overcomes every fear, every doubt, even when there seems no way out."[14]

I eventually ran my second marathon with a 76-minute personal record qualifying for the Boston Marathon with a 7-minute cushion. The ENTIRE 21 months that separated my first and second marathon was essential in building mental, physical, and spiritual stamina. It also helped me gain a better perspective. There's a bigger picture. There's a higher purpose. Trust the plan and let patience, through trials, have her perfect work. Roads to the most magnificent views have the most bumps. Raise your hands and take it in stride."[15]

Open-Handed, Open-Hearted, Open-Minded

Open-Handed - We discussed change a fair amount in chapter 4. Openness is more than accepting and adjusting with change. Being open and receptive to what God has for you comes through a trust to where you can say out loud with confidence, "I know you want to do me good."[16] Being open-handed is generosity that gives much more than just money that will be no more someday. Give of yourself by commending the talents of others and celebrating their abilities. Encouragement is one way you can be generous to people of any age. **Help create the future potential of others.**

Open-Hearted - We know to guard our heart, for everything we do flows from it.[17] We let people in; we keep evil out. Jesus loves people, yet hates sin. We are created for relationship with God and one another. We were never meant to do life alone, stop trying! **Connect with people on a personal level; you are worth knowing.** Let that sink in. You can afford to love other people unconditionally. Take the time to understand who they are. Interacting with people diminishes obstacles and produces opportunities for fulfillment. God creates so many unique and beautiful individuals. There are billions to meet. Get busy.

Open-Minded - Whether you have traveled extensively or very little, there is an entire world with many new ideas and different ways of doing things. In east Texas lingo, "There is more than one way to skin a cat." Some new ideas will honestly provide a better way of thinking and quality of life. Be accepting of ways God wants to lead you down new paths. **Choose Christ, cultivate friendships, and develop new mindsets.**

Strategic Solutions

- When there is a smile in your heart, it shows on your face.
- *Viction* is the euphoria of seeing a vision, with action steps for the process ahead.
- You have the unique ability to choose in your heart what you believe about yourself.
- When entering a space, it helps to clean from left to right. Order avoids retracing steps, and progress is apparent in a short amount of time.
- Random thoughts use energy continuously, like open apps on a cell phone. When multiple apps are running at once, the battery drains much quicker. Close the apps in your mind. Mental clarity requires focus.
- Organization in and of itself is not the end goal; it is the springboard for higher productivity and an enjoyable life where you do not have to keep redoing fundamental things over and over again.
- Look for the opportunities; they are all around you.
- The little extra attention to detail with the right motive can be a game-changer in ways you never thought possible.
- Our lack of *viction* may very well be blocking incredible opportunities God wants us to see and access.
- We have an infinite God who is not bound by our puny limitations.
- Life is not about limitations; it is about optimization. Change your vantage point.
- Make "the ask." God is just waiting to fling doors wide open for you, His favorite child.
- Situations do not define you, your choices do.
- Go after your goals and dreams with great resolve.
- Help create the future potential of others.

Viction: Where Vision and Action Collide

- Connect with people on a personal level; YOU are worth knowing.
- Choose Christ, cultivate friendships, and develop new mindsets.

Cheering You On & Championing His Call!

Divine Insight
Choosing Christ & Cultivating Friendship:
_____
_____

Victionary Insight
Communicating Vision & Combining Action:
_____
_____

Team Insight
Connecting People & Creating Potential:
_____
_____

Young Leader Insight
Commending Talents & Celebrating Abilities:
_____
_____

Generational KidMin Insight
Cultivating Relationships & Collaborating Mentorships:
_____
_____

NAVIGATING NOTEWORTHINESS

CHAPTER 8

N - Navigating Noteworthiness

Let your reasonableness be known to everyone. The Lord is at hand; do not be anxious about anything, but in everything by prayer and supplication with thanksgiving let your requests be made known to God. And the peace of God, which surpasses all understanding will guard your hearts and your minds in Christ Jesus. Finally, brothers, whatever is true, whatever is honorable, whatever is just, whatever is pure, whatever is lovely, whatever is commendable, if there is any excellence, if there is anything worthy of praise, think about these things.[1]

"We must be careful not to confuse activity with accomplishment."[2]

New, Noble, and Notable

New - Our Heavenly Father loves diversity; just look at the difference between a giraffe and a monkey. Both unique in appearance with different qualities and capabilities. The terrain is diverse, even within regions and indeed throughout the world. God creates things that never existed before. Discoveries seem to be limitless.

We like new and different. One glance down a cereal or soft drink aisle will show you a variety of choices for the same product and often even within the same brand. Coca Cola keeps rolling out new first-time taste experiences for its consumers. In the Coke soft drink line alone, there is Coca Cola, Diet Coke, Coke Zero, Sugar Coca-Cola Life, Cherry Coke, Caffeine Free Diet Coke, Vanilla Coke, and Coke Zero Sugar Cherry. Man loves to create new things, just like our Maker.[3]

The question we need to ask ourselves is the "why" behind the new. Coca-Cola is interested in selling you a product for consumption now. In life, ministry, education, and business, the new must be of significance. **We need not find a new message, instead find new ways to present THE timeless message.** Each believer has a personal and corporate responsibility to help the lost come to know and experience Jesus Christ. Salvation is not the end; rather, the beginning of new life.

I have seen it time and again, especially in third world countries. They find Jesus and are not ashamed to start teaching the moment they know about Him. Then they learn a new verse and are sharing it with all of their might to anyone who will listen. Lose the timidity and intimidation that others may know more than you. Start afresh and anew right now. Share what you know and learn together with others. **Teach what you know to grow.**

Noble - Know your rank and your place as an individual and as a leader. You are seated high above powers and principalities at the right hand of God. There is no reason to slump or look down at the ground. As a lover of God and Jesus follower, you have the noblest spirit of all flowing through the very core and depths of your being. Rise oh sleepyhead and know your place. Occupy the space God generously granted to you before he fashioned you in your mother's womb. Be eager and settle for nothing less than God's best! Here is an excellent example of being noble and the look of nobility. *Now these Jews were more noble than those in Thessalonica; they received the word with all eagerness, examining the Scriptures daily to see if these things were so.*[4]

Viction: Where Vision and Action Collide

You have been gifted with exceptional personal qualities to cultivate. The highest moral principles and ideas live in you because of the immutable, infallible word of God of which makes you tick. Rise oh son and daughter of Zion. Hear the spiritual trumpet's blast as you bring glory to the Father and praise to the Son. DO NOT let the world reduce you to stinking thinking. Deliberately think on this, *but he who is noble plans noble things, and on noble things he stands.*[5]

Notable - NOTHING about you is ordinary. You are a one-of-a-kind creation. No one else has your exact DNA or thumbprint. Your very life is to be the highest form of a living recommendation letter written by Jesus. The spirit of the living God writes on the pages of your moldable and pliable heart. Someone just questioned these previous two sentences. Was it you? Feast on 2 Corinthians 3:2-3 as it is evident. *For your very lives are our "letters of recommendation," permanently engraved on our hearts, recognized and read by everybody. As a result of our ministry, you are living letters written by Christ, not with ink but by the Spirit of the living God - not carved onto stone tablets but on the tablets of tender hearts.*[6]

Your nobility makes confessions like this. I submit myself to God, along with anything that seems to be holding me back. Therefore, I succeed in being myself. I stop looking at what I cannot do and look at everything I can do from this moment forward. Because I am a child of God and follow His example, I call things that are not as though they are.[7] Therefore, I help make projects successful. I curate opportunities. I am on the best teams and have lots of fun living life! **I seize opportunities for tomorrow because my Heavenly Father is all-knowing and gives me foresight.**

Networking Now

Twelve years ago, I went on my first trip to Rwanda with Diana Wiley and two other women. We went to help ten widows of the Genocide against the Tutsi, most living with HIV/Aids and their families. We took funds to purchase two sheep, shear the sheep, and start teaching the ladies how to spin wool with wooden drop spindles so they could earn income for themselves and their children. Vision and action are in place for this moment to become a movement. There was unknowingly so much to learn.

Over the years, Diana, founder and executive director of True Vineyard Ministries, willingly and steadily kept growing in her knowledge of sheep, fiber, and business in Rwanda. There are now three hundred sheep who provide wool for 123 at-risk women who work their way out of poverty and overcome trauma. What began as True Vineyard Ministries with the employment of ten women has now become the number one employer of women in the Musanze District of Rwanda known as Handspun Hope.[8]

Although the learning curve has been tremendous, Diana kept going back to God and asking the 'what if' questions. We had the opportunity to visit after her recent trip to Rwanda. We reminisced about the women, and the sheep for a moment. Then Diana said, the story about the rabbits is just as crazy as the sheep. Wanting to hear the whole story, Diana began.

She was at a fiber show in Seguin, Texas, where Angora yarn was selling. She watched the people spinning the wool as it was coming off the rabbits. With a green light from God, Diana pursued information, and within a matter of weeks, funds for the rabbits were received in full. Within months Diana drove to Missouri to purchase three German Angora rabbits for $300 apiece to take to Rwanda. The rabbits would provide another source of raw materials for the women to earn additional income. Two females and one buck were off for an adventure with delightful Diana. The rabbit hutches were specially designed with tile roofs for a more calming effect than tin during the rainy season in Rwanda. They even went through an international inspection by USADA on Diana's back porch in San Marcos before everyone could depart from the states.

It sounds easy enough, purchase the bunnies and hop on an airline. Yet it took involving the Rwanda Agriculture Board for the rabbits to enter the country. Through a series of mishaps, they could not fly on one airline due to an embargo at the time. Then transit permits had to be acquired for Kenya. The rabbits were to be on a flight without dogs, and the list of complications kept mounting.

Diana missed a flight because additional restrictions come into play on how the rabbits could travel. Diana had to build another cage in the Air Cargo section of the Houston airport. She went to Home Depot quickly to get the necessary supplies to make an inset for an additional enclosure. After all of this, the rabbits flew out of the country on a separate flight before Diana. She caught up with Master Adam, Momma Evie, and Momma Alice, the rabbit trio in Heathrow. Then they all flew to Nairobi. Diana claimed the rabbits in Nairobi and took them to a hotel for the night, where they happily scamper around. The next day they went back to the airport to fly into Rwanda, where the rabbits came out through the baggage claim with the luggage.

Rabbits are typically prolific. However, for fifteen long months, there was not a single baby born. During this time, Momma Evie got a tooth infection. She spent six weeks with a veterinarian trying to get rid of her tooth infection. Momma Evie died. Now there is one male and one female rabbit.

After a rather long wait where God said yes to this new initiative, Momma Alice had four males, one died. Then she had twelve more. The young rabbits have had babies, and the Angora rabbit population established in Rwanda is in affiliation with the International German Angora Rabbit Association. These "Rwabbits" help provide another revenue stream for women.

Hope is the primary vehicle for change. Today Handspun Hope employs 123 women who support 527 family members. One hundred eighty-one children are receiving an education. Never underestimate what God is doing when you say, "Yes, Lord." Navigating noteworthiness is done through networking in the now moments where *viction* takes place. We are to do life, ministry, education, and business together.

Necessary Necessities

We have these precious few moments in time to advance the kingdom of God. Lists are highly over-rated, so I step cautiously into sharing multiple areas where basic principles will shape and accelerate foundational leadership development as few things will. Spend time allowing the Holy Spirit to quicken you in areas where further attention to detail is needed. We increase capacity in the Secret Place with the Most High God.

Bring God into every equation. Invite Jesus into every situation. Learn more trust as God will show and tell you tremendous and mighty things to come. God speaks from the inside out not the outside in. Hear Him with new ears. God is not irritated with you or frustrated with the process. Refuse to talk at Him; fellowship with Him.

Be willing to change quickly. Die daily to self. God will not trump your self-will. He is asking you to lay it down. When is the last time you bowed on bended knee and/or laid yourself to the floor to encounter the very presence of Jesus? If you can't remember when, it's been too long. Burn with passion for God and refuse to be engrossed with the things of this world. Be open to the ways of God you do not understand. Seek the evidence of God's presence with an attitude of expectancy.

Shun perfectionism. For it is a spirit that is always doing something without ever resting. Perfectionism nullifies grace, replaces joy with pride and self-righteousness. This spirit views everything in light of a pass/fail or black and white lenses. Perfectionism is hard on yourself and everyone else because the performance-based race is never-ending.

Exchange lies for the truth. It goes like this. Change your thinking; then, it changes your feeling, which in turn changes how you act. Later double check your belief system. What lies have you come into agreement with for the sake of false humility? The exchange rate is high; do it now; make the exchange of lies for the truth.

Respect Boundaries. Respect the boundaries you have set for yourself, and those others have in place for their life too. Don't break confidence. Everyone's life is a testimony in the making. Protect yourself and all the individuals involved when you know sensitive information. Listen more than you speak.

Don't give up so easily. There is a place of resistance where personal growth and learning take place in this type of incubator better than any other circumstance in life. An overcoming inheritance takes place in this arena. When we refuse to give up, we make Satan pay forever, trying to touch us.

Operate in an Overcoming Anointing. Desire to be a God and Kingdom influencer. Speak the Word and pray for the result. Read the Bible to your experiences, not vice-versa. Growth is a lifestyle. Rather than expecting a revival, be the revival.

Note the Negotiables

Never negotiate the word of God, His character, or principles. Make a note of areas you can negotiate within reason in small incremental steps. God has given you personal resources to steward, including time, money, energy, and creativity.

In negotiations with people, look for every opportunity where a "win-win" can happen relationally. Most issues are problematic. **Think through a variety of options that can be beneficial for everyone before making a significant decision.** Avoid short-term wins and focus on long-term gains by keeping the end in mind. Avoid using the words "you" and "I." Stick to first-person plural pronouns with the terms we, our, and us to promote a teamwork approach to the decision-making process. Focus on common areas of interest and work from there. Always search for ways to add value.

> Collect successes daily; there are no small wins.

Navigating Noteworthiness

As our initial time together comes to a close, I am writing you an encouraging note on ways to handle noteworthiness you experience in more significant degrees. Your desire to maximize *viction* will undoubtedly catapult you into new realms of fulfilling success. God will surely increase your territory as you look to Him, the author and finisher of your faith.[9]

Dearest Victorious Victioneer,

Connect with people on a personal level; YOU are worth knowing. You have the unique ability to choose in your heart what you believe about yourself. Recognize you are your only limitation. Remember, excessiveness in any area is a precursor for covering up personal insecurities. It's OK to let go of insecurities. Conquer your past by focusing on the future. Embrace who you are. Your life is not about limitations; it is about optimization. For what is impossible with people is possible with God.[10]

Check your thinking frequently as your thoughts proceed your words. Random thoughts use energy continuously, like open apps on a cell phone. When multiple apps are running at once, the battery drains much quicker. Close the apps in your mind. Mental clarity requires focus. Both success and failure can be traced to whatever you think and do daily.

When given a compliment, say thank you and show gratitude with genuine sincerity. Then give all the glory back to God as quickly as possible. Do this as an act of worship from you unto the Father in the Secret Place. For apart from Jesus, you are nothing.[11]

Situations that cause you anger and pain are the very things you are to change. Never be afraid to make a big "ask." The right question can give you incredible access with uncommon and unprecedented favor. Collect successes daily; there are no small wins. Part of life's celebration is in the actual process of preparation. Therefore, learn to measure what you treasure. Then recognize and refuse to dwell on those things beyond your control.

Have enough passion for Jesus that you have compassion for others. Relevant leadership is about communicating well. Therefore, listen before you speak. Be prepared to engage with others regarding their thoughts and concerns without picking up an offense. Help people discover where God's moving even when there's pain associated with the growth inside of you.

Meet individuals where they are and help them get to where they want to go. People are starving for someone to come alongside them to lighten the load. Willingly help others develop a blueprint to follow so they can experience success. God is doing the same for you even now.

Become conscious of the seasons in life. Guard your heart. Identity can quickly become attached to a person or what you do instead of who you belong to and everything you are in Christ. Understand that transitions are the most undertaught and overlooked processes in leadership. Learn about change, *for it is how you will reorient and go from how something used to be to how it is in the current moment.*

Get honest with yourself; there is probably an area of life where you are experiencing some form of transition even now. How you think and react to finality is paramount in how you will enter a new season. Be bold. Be brave. The Lord, our God, is with you.

Embrace God-given time-out moments as they serve as reset buttons. There are periods where God will deliberately get you to a sit and soak place. Be content with this season. His personal touch makes ALL the difference where vision and action collide. For out of it is a birthing of something far more significant than you have previously known or experienced. It is in these moments where we discover viction, the euphoria of seeing a vision, with action steps for the process ahead.

Cheering you on as you champion His call,
Sherry

Strategic Solutions

- We need not find a new message, instead find a new way to present THE timeless message.
- Teach what you know to grow.
- Biblical leadership is being grounded in your theology while being innovative with technology.
- I seize opportunities for tomorrow because my Heavenly Father is all-knowing and gives me foresight.
- Bring God into every equation.
- Be willing to change quickly.
- Shun perfectionism.
- Exchange lies for the truth.
- Respect boundaries.
- Operate in an overcoming anointing.
- Never negotiate the word of God, His character, or principles. Make a note of areas you can negotiate within reason in small incremental steps.
- Think through a variety of options that can be beneficial for everyone before making a significant decision.
- Collect successes daily; there are no small wins.
- Be prepared to engage with others regarding their thoughts and concerns without picking up an offense.
- Help people develop a blueprint to follow so they can experience success.
- Biblical leadership is being grounded in theology while being innovative with technology.
- When given a compliment, say thank you with genuine sincerity. Then be quick to provide all the glory back to God as quickly as possible. Do this as an act of worship from you unto the Father, for without Him, we are nothing.

Cheering You On & Championing His Call!

Divine Insight
Choosing Christ & Cultivating Friendship:
_____
_____

Victionary Insight
Communicating Vision & Combining Action:
_____
_____

Team Insight
Connecting People & Creating Potential:
_____
_____

Young Leader Insight
Commending Talents & Celebrating Abilities:
_____
_____

Generational KidMin Insight
Cultivating Relationships & Collaborating Mentorships:
_____
_____

APPENDIX A

Do you know Jesus?

If you are reading this page, then you recognize that you can't handle life on your own and you're seeking help that will make a real difference. Perhaps you're reading this because your not certain if you can answer "yes" to this question, "Are you a Christian?"

1. **Admit that you have sinned and made mistakes.** *For all have sinned; and come short of the glory of God* (Romans 3:23 KJV).
2. **Know that you owe a debt you cannot pay, but God has made a way.** *For the wages of sin is death; but the gift of God is eternal life through Jesus Christ our Lord* (Romans 6:23 KJV).
3. **God really loves you and Jesus canceled your debt.** *But God demonstrates His own love toward us, in that while we were still sinners, Christ died for us. Since we have now been justified by his blood, how much more shall we be saved from God's wrath through him* (Romans 5:8-9 NKJV).
4. **Believe in Jesus and trust in God.** *If you confess with your mouth the Lord Jesus and believe in your heart that God has raised Him from the dead, you will be saved* (Romans 10:9 NKJV).
5. **Ask Jesus to live and take up residence in your heart.** *With the heart one believes unto righteousness,*

and with the mouth confession is made unto salvation (Romans 10:9 NKJV).
6. **Receive the greatest gift of all.** *For whoever calls on the name of the LORD shall be saved* (Romans 10:13).

Talk to God – Father, I admit my desperate need for you. I have sinned and my sins have separated me from you. Please forgive me of my sins and help me to turn away from my former conduct. I believe that your Son, Jesus died for my sins and arose from the grave in victory, power and might. Jesus, I ask you to come into my heart and live. Take up residence in my life to rule and reign. Fill me with your Holy Spirit and power. I receive you as Lord and Savior of my life. Thank You for saving me and setting me free.

Knowing Jesus – What's Next?

Believe and Speak It – *Tell someone about your decision to repent of your sins and ask Jesus Christ into your heart.* Repent means to turn away from and go in the opposite direction of your former conduct.

Take Action – *Spend time getting to know God each and every day.* He's been waiting for this opportunity. Talk to Him and let Him speak to you through His Word.

If you don't have a hard copy of the Bible, there are internet links to free online versions to view. One source is http://www.biblegateway.com.

Get in a good Bible based church that believes in the power of Almighty God. Learn of God by listening to sound teaching.

Get Baptized – This is a physical act of obedience. As you are immersed in water, you are buried with Christ and raised again to newness of life. Getting baptized is a public display of the decision you made in your heart to make Jesus Lord and Savior of your life.

NOURISHING NOTES

Introduction
1. Deuteronomy 4:14, 8:11; Isaiah 28:13
2. Isaiah 35:4; Daniel 10:19

Chapter One
1. Psalm 139:5-6 TPT
2. William D. Greenman, *Discover Your Purpose! Design Your Destiny! Direct Your Achievement!: Proven Strategies for a Productive, God-Centered Life!* (Shippensburg, PA: Destiny Image Publishers, 1998), 231, quote by Joel Author Baker
3. Matthew 6:6
4. Matthew 6:33
5. Psalm 46:5 NIV
6. John 3:16
7. 1 Corinthians 2:16
8. Matthew 19:26
9. Psalm 75:6-7
10. Isaiah 55:8-9
11. 1 Timothy 6:6
12. Romans 12:19
13. 1 Samuel 30:1-20
14. Ruth 1
15. James 1:5
16. Eva M. Krockow, Ph.D., "How Many Decisions Do We Make Each Day?" posted September 27, 2018, https://www.psychologytoday.com/us/blog/stretching-theory/201809/how-many-decisions-do-we-make-each-day.
17. United Conference Featuring John Maxwell and John Bevere at the LETU Belcher Center, Longview Texas September 12, 2019 at 7:00 PM
18. 1 Corinthians 9: 19, 22b-23
19. 1 Corinthians 9:23 TPT

Chapter Two

1. Ezra 10:4 NIV
2. talks/membership_by_c._s._lewis.txt · Last modified: 2014/01/14 18:28 by grant.
3. Psalm 75:6-7
4. Genesis 1:12
5. Exodus 20:12
6. Isaiah 5:20
7. Romans 13:1 NIV
8. Hebrews 13:7, Colossians 3:18, Ephesians 6:1
9. 2 Chronicles 7:14
10. 1 Timothy 2:1-2, 1 Peter 2:17
11. Jim Harter, *"Employment Engagement on the Rise in the U.S."* August 26, 2018, https://news.gallup.com/poll/241649/employee-engagement-rise.aspx.
12. Matthew 5:19
13. Deuteronomy 25:15 NIV
14. The Way Bible Church (TWBC) Workflow Chart, created by Dr. Joel Tiemeyer.
15. 2 Timothy 3:16
16. 2 Corinthians 4:7
17. James 4:2b
18. Acts 8:1-3
19. Caleb Parke, "Chinese Christians jailed for faith memorize Bible because guards 'can't take what's hidden in your heart,'" *Fox News*, June 17, 2019, https://www.foxnews.com/faith-values/chinese-christians-imprisoned-for-faith-memorize-bible-guards-cant-take-whats-hidden-in-your-heart.
20. Luke 6:22
21. Philippians 2:3
22. 1 Corinthians 15:57

Chapter Three

1. John 15:16
2. John C. Maxwell, *The Choice Is Yours: Today's Decisions for the Rest of Your Life* (Cape Town: Struik Christian Gifts, 2016), 124.
3. Genesis 6:8 - The Living Bible Translation
4. Genesis 6:8 - KJV, NLT
5. Genesis 6:8 - AMP, NKJV
6. Proverbs 12:13, 13:3
7. Mike Murdock, *Leadership Secrets for Excellence & Increase* (Dallas,

8. TX: Wisdom International, 1997), 22.
8. *Ibid.*
9. Beth Moore, *So Long, Insecurity: You've Been a Bad Friend to Us* (Carol Stream, IL: Tyndale House Publishers, Inc., 2016), 85.
10. Philippians 3:13
11. Revelation 12:10
12. Isaiah 28:10 KJV
13. Ephesians 6:8
14. https://www.chastitymarie.com
15. Stephen M. R. Covey and Rebecca R. Merrill, *The Speed of Trust: The One Thing That Changes Everything* (New York, NY: Free Press, 2018), 62.
16. *Ibid.*
17. Joyce Meyer, *The Love Revolution* (London: Hodder & Stoughton, 2010), 10.
18. Ephesians 5:11

Chapter Four

1. Isaiah 43:19 NIV
2. Smith Wigglesworth, *Smith Wigglesworth Devotional* (New Kensington, PA: Whitaker House, 1999), 35.
3. Philippians 4:7, John 14:27
4. Psalm 34:5
5. Stephen R. Covey, *The 7 Habits of Highly Effective People* (London: Simon & Schuster, 2005).
6. "What does the Bible say about confidence," GotQuestions.org, https://www.gotquestions.org/Bible-confidence.html.
7. Philippians 1:6 ASV
8. Romans 10:11
9. Romans 8:31
10. Mark 6:50
11. "2293.tharseo," Bible Hub, Strong's Concordance, accessed January 2, 2020, https://biblehub.com/greek/2293.htm.
12. 2 Kings 18:5
13. Esther 4:14
14. Patty Pasion, "Philippines top global source of child pornography – Unicef," updated December 13, 2017, https://www.rappler.com/nation/191219-philippines-top-global-source-child-pornography-unicef.
15. https://www.barna.com/research/top-10-releases-of-2019/.
16. Patrick Van Kessel, "10 Facts about Americans and YouTube,"

https://www.pewresearch.org/fact-tank/2019/12/04/10-facts-about-americans-and-youtube/.

[17] Carey Nieuwhof, *"DIDNT SEE IT COMING: Overcoming the Seven Greatest Challenges That No One Expects and Everyone Experiences,"* (Colorado Springs: Waterbrook, 2018).

Chapter Five

[1] Habakkuk 2:1-3
[2] Russ Busby, Laura Georgakakos, *Billy Graham: God's Ambassador: A Lifelong Mission of Giving Hope to the World* (Alexandria, VA: Time Life Books, 1999), 65.
[3] William Bridges Associates, https://wmbridges.com/what-is-transition/.
[4] William Bridges Associates, https://wmbridges.com.
[5] https://www.ecfvp.org/tools/72/understanding-the-theory-of-change-and-transition.
[6] *Ibid.*
[7] *Overcomers*, a movie release by Sony Pictures through its label Affirm Films, August 23, 2019.
[8] https://www.ecfvp.org/tools/72/understanding-the-theory-of-change-and-transition.
[9] *Ibid.*

Chapter Six

[1] Titus 2:7-8 NIV
[2] Heidi and Roland Baker, *Reckless Devotion*, (Ada, MI: Chosen Books, 2014), 11.
[3] John Maxwell and Jim Dornan, *Becoming a Person of Influence: How to Positively Impact the Lives of Others* (Nashville, TN: Harper Collins Leadership, 2018).
[4] Edgar Dale Cone of Influence.
[5] Isaiah 28:10
[6] Hook - grown dendrites https://www.teachhub.com/discover-teaching-strategies-individualize-instruction.
[7] Gary D. Chapman and Jocelyn Green, *The 5 Love Languages: The Secret to Love That Lasts* (Chicago: Northfield Publishing, 2017).
[8] *Ibid.*
[9] Hebrews 4:16
[10] 1 Corinthians 1:9

Chapter Seven

1. Deuteronomy 31:6
2. Deborah Smith Pegues, *30 Days to Taming Your Tongue: What You Say (and Don't Say) Will Improve Your Relationships* (New York: MJF Books, 2013), 112.
3. Proverbs 13:12
4. Matthew 6:26-34
5. Romans, 8:28, John 10:10
6. Luke 6:45
7. Proverbs 24:3
8. Psalms 119:9
9. Exodus 20:12
10. Proverbs 27:10 New Century Version
11. Galatians 6:10
12. Titus 3:2
13. Romans 12:18
14. www.lelamaemusic.com
15. Instagram @jenrunsup
16. Jeremiah 32:41
17. Proverbs 4:23

Chapter Eight

1. Philippians 4:5-8
2. Rick Howard and Jamie Lash, *This Was Your Life!: Preparing to Meet God Face to Face* (Ada, MI: Chosen Books, 1998), 132.
3. www.worldofcocacola.com
4. Act 17:11
5. Isaiah 32:8
6. 2 Corinthians 3:2-3 TPT
7. Ephesians 5:1 and Romans 4:17
8. Amy Brinkerhoff, "One Step at a Time," True Vineyard Ministries, https://www.truevineyard.org/featured-stories/2019/8/26/one-step-at-a-time.
9. Hebrews 12:2
10. Luke 18:27
11. John 15:5

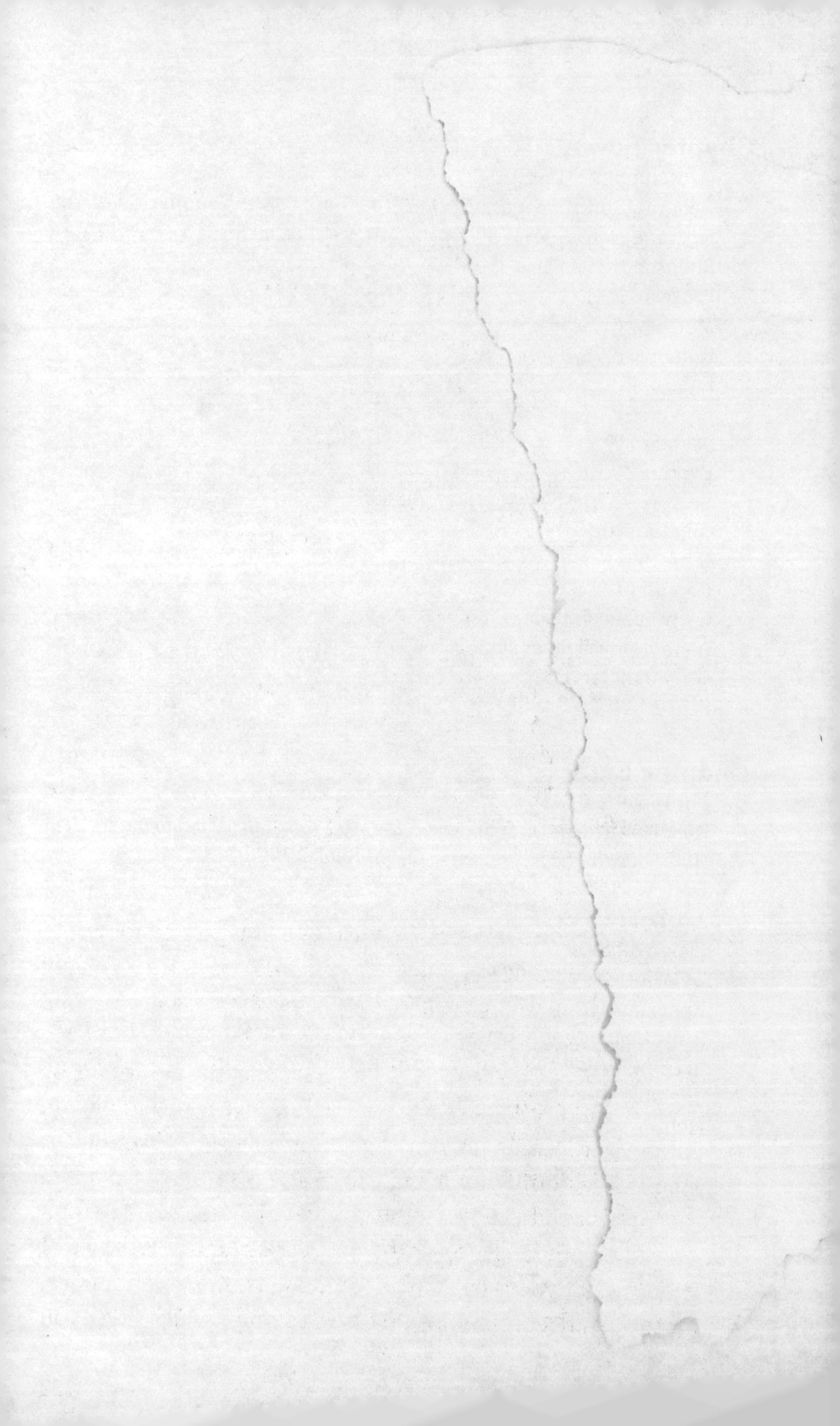

APPRECIATIVE ACKNOWLEDGEMENTS

Writing is much more than what you know or experience. It represents the lives of many individuals who have written chapters or pages on my heart and impacted life significantly as a community.

I am thankful for the memories of Lela Mae Alexander, a maternal grandmother and Opal Brinlee, a most precious Momma who modeled leadership quietly in the mundane activities of daily living where they embraced joy and continuously made time for me. I am also forever grateful and gladly honor the mentor and accountability partner I have in the lovely Lynda Davidson, my sweet sister-friend forever and always.

Marvelous Maxie Chester, my beloved late husband. I am incredibly grateful for your relentless encouragement for me to step out in faith. Your support in every endeavor is a gift I truly cherish. Oh, how this would thrill you as it represents lessons learned together and countless discussions on how to lead well. Thankful for Jim Chester and Dusty Sheffield, my adult kids by choice, who depict leadership. We are, I am very proud of you.

To my four Dearest Darling Daughters, Jennifer Wenneker, Shery Huddleston, Allie Thompson, and Kimberly Garrard, you all are indeed my sunshine. I love you dearly, like you a lot, and have fun laughing with you. As our "Little Women," I am thankful for your strong work ethic, sense of independence, adventure, and compassion. This "Marmee" will "like you forever and love you for always." Thank you for seeing me as the woman God has called me to be, and graciously overlooking my shortcomings in the meanwhile.

Super thankful for my work family, the incredible staff at The Way Bible Church. Joel Tiemeyer, your leadership, mentorship, and friendship are invaluable. Derrick Dillion, Jeff Tiemeyer, Damon Wilks, and Chad Kopal, your sphere of influence, is far-reaching; Hunter Elliott, and Korey Hankins, you are my favorite younger leaders with great ideas and generational Kidmin insight. I learn from you often. Bonnie Tiemeyer, Rachael Johnson, Sheri Tiemeyer, and Amy Tiemeyer, you are women of faith in whom I cherish much. Thank you for being my people. I appreciate you all walking with me through the valley of the shadow of death this past year. It is an honor to do life and serve with such outstanding sacrificial leaders.

To the Elders and my church family at The Way Bible Church, you continue to amaze me with your heart for children and outreach. I am grateful for your continual encouragement and support. Your lovingkindness is precious to me. To the teacher leaders, volunteers, grands, and coaches of TWBC KIDS, you are outstanding in how you love, play, and engage with children. You have my utmost respect and adoration. I am in awe of the fantastic job you do every week.

A special thanks to the Behind-the Scenes Team of Cris Millsap, Vickie Jenkins, Amy Goldsmith and Taffy Tigieser. Your prophetic words, prayers, support, encouragement, and willingness to do major "grunt" work is nothing short of outstanding. Thank you for doing life with me on so many levels and bringing life to countless projects.

Vicki Dietz, you are a Godsend. Thank you for editing and lending your creative talents to help this book come to fruition. Your strength of character and diligence is admirable.

Joel Tiemeyer, Betty Lawson and Lynda Davidson, I appreciate your editorial insights.

Jeremy Wenneker, I genuinely appreciate your Web Page

development and making technical things look doable for me. Your commitment to excellence is noteworthy in all aspects of life.

Martijn and Amy Van Tilborough, Ryan and Beth Frank, Trish Weeks, Ricardo Miller, and Esther Moreno, you dreamed with me and believed in me when things were just an idea in the making. I appreciate your creative genius and continuous support. Ricardo, you are an exceptional coach and mentor; thank you.

There are ladies in leadership who have molded and shaped my life in specific ways, their skill sets, read throughout these pages. Special thanks to Lynda Davidson, Esther Moreno, Trish Weeks, Bonnie Tiemeyer, Patsy Bolton, Joan Petty, Nina Williams, Pat Murray, Betty Lawson, Sherry McGraw, Kay McClure, Connie Mabe, Shelley Patterson, Judy Tipping, Hillary Young, Sharon Derrick, Cynthia Bayuk-Bishop, Karen Whitacker, Elaine Ballard, Becky Clapp, and Carol Henderson.

To those who worked in children's ministry, youth ministry, and bus ministry at First Baptist Church in Sulphur Springs, Texas, as I grew up, I want to say thank you. I appreciate the time you spent preparing, teaching, and reaching out to me and other kids like me who needed someone to believe in them with unconditional acceptance.

To all of those whose names are not mentioned, yet have written on the pages of my heart. Thank you for conversations and shared life's experiences. I am fortunate to know you.

May your lives be forever blessed.

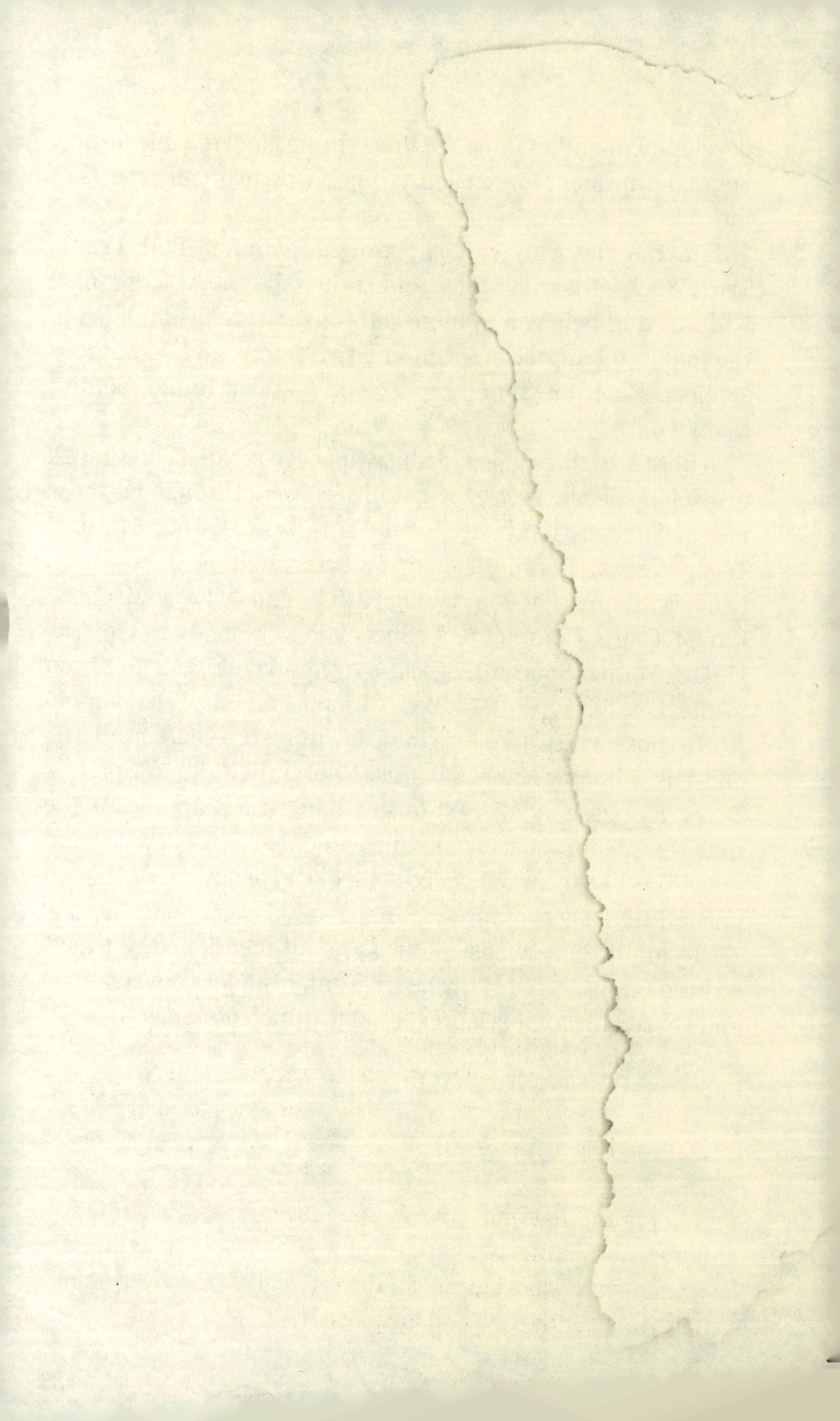

ABOUT THE AUTHOR

Sherry Chester is the Children's Pastor at The Way Bible Church in Sulphur Springs, Texas. Sherry is passionate about training leaders, kids, and families on any continent to live and lead well.

Sherry holds a Master of Science in Educational Administration and a Master of Arts in Theology. Sherry is a graduate from The School of Supernatural Children's Ministry through Kids in Ministry International and earned a diploma in Children's Ministry from Kidmin Academy.

Sherry taught Special Education and English in a 1A school district. She established Head Start for two 4A systems. Sherry led in a 5A district through federal programs, wrote and administered grants, coordinated emergency preparedness, and served as Director of Professional Development for 27 years.

Sherry and late husband Maxie have six successful adult children, four wonderful sons-in-law, one lovely daughter-in-law, and fifteen smart grandchildren. She likes to travel, enjoys people, interior design, and ping pong!

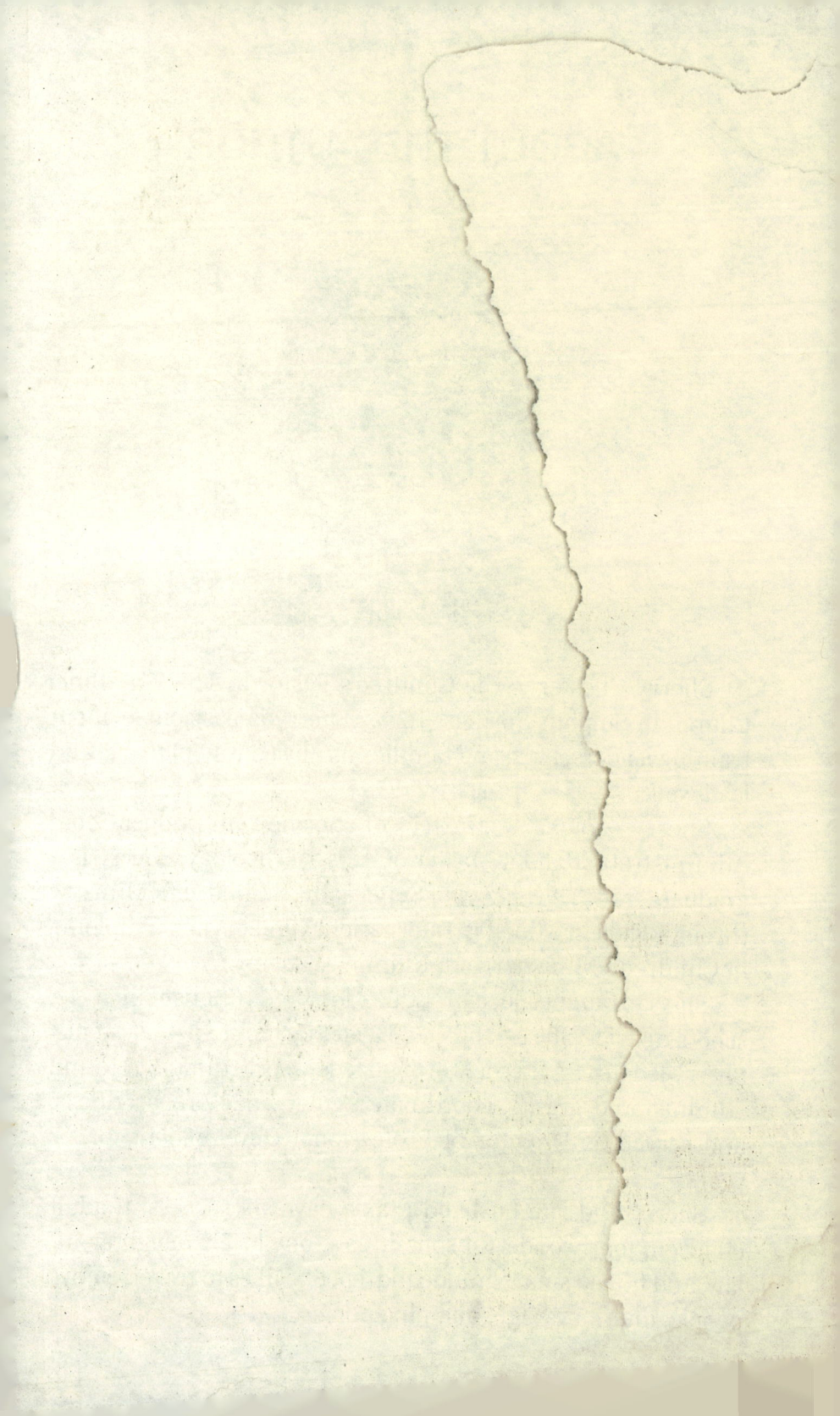